A JOURNEY
BACK
TO NATURE

A JOURNEY BACK TO NATURE

A HISTORY OF
STRATHCONA
PROVINCIAL PARK

CATHERINE MARIE GILBERT

Heritage House Publishing Company Ltd.
heritagehouse.ca

Cataloguing information available from Library and Archives Canada
978-1-77203-358-8 (pbk)
978-1-77203-359-5 (ebook)

Edited by Audrey McClellan
Cover and interior book design by Setareh Ashrafologhalai
Cover image: A colourized image of beautiful Della Lake,
Image PN0066 Alberni Valley Museum Photograph Collection

The interior of this book was produced on FSC®-certified, acid-free paper, processed chlorine free and printed with vegetable-based inks.

Heritage House gratefully acknowledges that the land on which we live and work is within the traditional territories of the Lkwungen (Esquimalt and Songhees), Malahat, Pacheedaht, Scia'new, T'Sou-ke, and W̱SÁNEĆ (Pauquachin, Tsartlip, Tsawout, Tseycum) Peoples.

We acknowledge the financial support of the Government of Canada through the Canada Book Fund (CBF) and the Canada Council for the Arts, and the Province of British Columbia through the British Columbia Arts Council and the Book Publishing Tax Credit.

25 24 23 22 21   1 2 3 4 5

Printed in Canada

CONTENTS

FOREWORD

A S THE CURRENT BC Parks Area Supervisor responsible for managing Strathcona Park for the last eighteen years, and before that as an Extension Officer for five years, I am both humbled and honoured to be asked to write this foreword. Although there can only be one first, history is continually being formed, and having the opportunity to be part of Strathcona Park's history, with its notable label as BC's first provincial park, has often helped guide and inspire me, and I have taken pride over the years in maintaining and complementing its status by seeking out other firsts.

The knowledge of past events is important to society as it provides a foundation of who we are, where we have come from, and helps guide our present and future decisions. The saying "hindsight is 20/20" implies we may be able to understand something much better when assessed after the fact. However, the benefits of this can only be realized if historical facts are captured accurately and are not mere interpretations, personal opinions or manipulation through political will (government or public). Various people experiencing the same event at the same time may often have different opinions of the facts based on how they experienced it. They may all be completely honest and adamant in their recollection, and some or all recollections may be correct to some degree. This is what makes history writing difficult, as well as so important, and we must all leave room for considering other perspectives.

Government employees are mandated to be considerate and fair, listening and considering all perspectives prior to making or supporting a decision. Although government is often criticized, there is a process in place, and government works to learn all perspectives and gather information that will allow for making the most reasonable decision at any given time. Not every decision is correct, especially if viewed in hindsight, and few decisions, whatever the issue, will appeal to everyone, however it does mean that the Statutory Decision Makers do the best they can to reach a fair decision.

This brings us back to the importance of history and the benefits of having books like this developed and published. Catherine Gilbert has spent much time seeking out documents, assessing and comparing information and trying to confirm facts by cross referencing, interviewing and critical analysis. The history of Strathcona Park is filled with controversies and issues, which, if recorded accurately, are equally as important as all the good initiatives and stories to learn and prosper from.

While this book may not cover the complete detailed history of Strathcona Park—and I doubt any one book could—it does focus on key parts and provides what I believe to be a fair account of the times and events that I was around to witness or be part of.

You will read how the park has been plagued by resource extraction companies, both mining and logging, while also subjected to the impacts of hydro-electric development. However, those issues, while significant, may be rooted even further back, stemming from a historical land deal involving what could be argued as a "gifting" of much of Vancouver Island to Robert Dunsmuir under the E&N land grant. Perhaps another mistake may have been the lack of consideration of existing mineral claims prior to establishing the park, which ultimately set the stage for much public controversy surrounding amendments of regulations and legislation to accommodate industry or face legal challenges from industry.

Resource extraction issues aside, an alternative history could have easily resulted in different but significant impacts had the original vision of a "Banff-style" tourism development been realized.

What would we think of the impacts of multiple hotels, restaurants, stores, etc., along the shores of Buttle Lake, serviced by an endless stream of buses and cars on the roads, while the lake is covered with tour boats? As history has it, while the vision may have been a catalyst for creating the park in the first place, we fortunately don't have to consider all the challenges this would have brought.

NO HISTORICAL account today should ignore recognition of the Indigenous Peoples whose territories encompass the park. While the author understands this, more research is required, which she hopes to share in a future writing project. For the time being, let's all recognize their history and embrace their future involvement in the park.

As stated previously, history continues to be formed and therefore I would like to take this opportunity to recognize all those who in the past have voiced their opinions and lobbied for change when needed, both within the public and in the government. Having witnessed and experienced this passion and caring, I am confident that the future of Strathcona Park is bright and that it will remain the iconic park it is for all future generations.

ANDY SMITH
BC Parks Area Supervisor, Strathcona Provincial Park
March 2021

PREFACE

LTHOUGH WE celebrate the 110th anniversary of the founding of Strathcona Provincial Park in 2021, the triangle of land and water in mid-Vancouver Island that was delineated as a park in 1911 has a history going back into the mists of time. Indigenous Peoples of Vancouver Island have been coastal dwellers, and derive much of their sustenance from what they harvest along the coast and in the sea. We know, however, that they have always made forays into the inland mountainous regions, where evidence of marmot hunting and tools have been found. In an area that abounds with wildlife such as elk, deer and bear, these mammals were hunted too, especially in times when salmon were not as plentiful. The lakes of Vancouver Island abound with trout, a delicious addition to the diet. Recent archaeological evidence points to much more activity in the Park region than initially thought, such as tool making and butchering, changing notions of prehistory at today's Buttle Lake.

Numerous trails cross Vancouver Island that were travelled long before any Europeans found their way into these territories. Trade was conducted between peoples of the east coast of Vancouver Island and the west, and there was also interaction between western peoples and those who lived south of the present day Park.

The traditional use of what became Strathcona Provincial Park was not considered by those who wished to set aside this region as park land. The vision for the Park did not include wondering how it could be shared with the peoples who first ventured into the area, but rather was based on what white explorers beginning in the nineteenth century reported of their findings, and what excited the explorers was the idea of finding minerals.

It is interesting to think that the contradictions that were to plague the history of Strathcona Park are rooted in the very beginning of its establishment. The search for gold, which followed on the heels of the Cariboo gold rush in the British Columbia interior in the early 1860s, was uppermost in the minds of many, and when gold was found in the Strathcona region, out-of-work prospectors and placer miners were quick to try to exploit those discoveries. Initially, no one became wealthy on any of the nineteenth-century claims in Strathcona, but the die had been cast. Early-twentieth-century claims that existed when the Park was established would eventually allow for industrial-scale mining in the mid-1960s, in direct opposition to the stated purpose of setting aside this territory as park land.

There were complications, too, regarding pre-existing timber licences. Logging carried on within Park boundaries until the licences could be purchased, then commenced again when work began on an adjacent hydro-electric project. A portion of the old Esquimalt & Nanaimo land grant that bordered the Park was sold to logging concerns, and their activities on the edge of the Park and around Buttle Lake ruined the look of the approach to the Park.

This same part of the Park was considered for hydro-electric development, and changes were made to the original Park Act to allow for such development; however, the 1911 and 1929 plans did not come to fruition. A third consideration in the 1950s was abandoned for practical reasons, but also because of public protest against this use of the Park.

Legislation was changed again in the late 1950s to allow for a mine in the Park, but public protest would halt more industrial development when a second mine was proposed in the late 1980s. Lessons had been learned by some about just how destructive such an operation could be in a pristine territory, and this was not going to be allowed to happen again.

Finally, in 1993, a Master Plan was created which stated once and for all that Strathcona Provincial Park should be first and foremost a park for recreation, to be enjoyed by the public.

Today the Park is indeed enjoyed by many and with the addition of Forbidden Plateau on the east side in the 1960s, this region offers exceptional hiking, mountain climbing, boating and fishing opportunities, with nearby skiing in winter. It is still wild. Elk continue to roam through its forests, and cougars, deer, bears and marmots find their habitat there. The Park has its dangerous side and, sadly, hikers and mountain climbers, even those with vast experience, are lost in the Park every year. The public should certainly not be deterred from enjoying the wilderness experience of exploring this Park, but should enter the backcountry with the appropriate caution and equipment, and never alone.

In 1911 those who worked to establish the Park felt that people were looking for a journey back to nature, a chance to get away from the busyness of life and return to the era before the Industrial Revolution. Now, 110 years later, the desire to get back to nature has become increasingly important as people experience all the stresses related to technology and overcrowding. The onset of the COVID-19 virus in 2020 found ever more seekers of sanctuary in nature.

The Park provides a sanctuary, a place to reconnect with nature and consider our place in the universe. We can be grateful that some had the foresight to keep this region from permanent habitation by a human population, and even though industry was allowed to exploit its riches during some periods of its history, the Park continues to offer a unique sense of time standing still.

INTRODUCTION

I N A ROUGHLY triangular shape, Strathcona Provincial Park is situated approximately in the middle of Vancouver Island and comprises a territory of about 250,00 hectares, bordering Clayoquot Sound on the west, Port Alberni on the south side, and on the east, a large property that was once part of the Esquimalt and Nanaimo (E & N) land grant.[1] Today, with its majestic mountains and exceptional lakes and waterfalls, the Park is a premier destination for mountaineers, hikers, campers, fishers and paddlers, and provides an idyllic wilderness in which to get away from the vagaries of modern life. Yet behind this picture of serenity is a less than peaceful history, and Strathcona's borders would change numerous times throughout its history in favour of industrial development, prompting outbursts of discontent among conservationists.

The future of Strathcona Provincial Park looked promising in 1911, when Premier Richard McBride's Conservative government established the Park based upon reports by early explorers of its stunning vistas, rugged mountains, jewel-like lakes and magnificent waterfalls. There were lofty plans to transform this new park into the next Banff, with visions of rail lines extending 275 kilometres from Victoria to this remote location, and first-class accommodation awaiting travellers.

Neil S. Forkey, in his foreword to *Canadians and the Natural Environment to the Twenty-First Century*, writes that "Canadians' relationship with the natural world has been informed by two

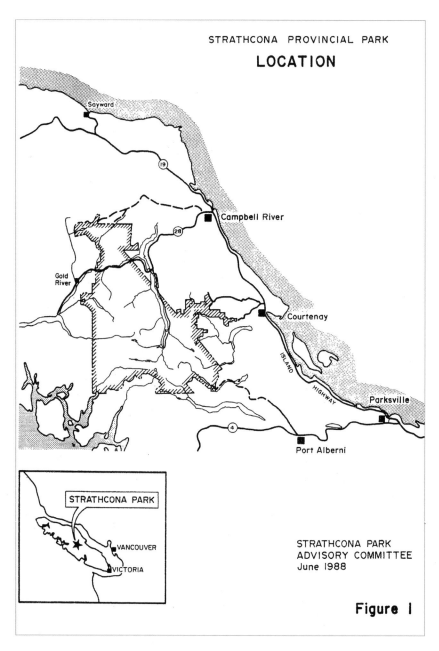

Location of Strathcona Provincial Park. MYRNA BOULDING COLLECTION

major impulses. The first is the need to exploit natural resources, while the second is the desire to protect them."[2]

Visions of erecting grand hotels, culling cougar populations, introducing non-native plant species to "beautify" the Park and even creating golf courses were all part of the plan. Park founders felt that with a little improvement, wilderness areas could be made attractive to visitors.

Park boundaries were drawn in straight lines, without taking into consideration contours of land or bodies of water. Buttle Lake's northeast corner was cut off, so the lake was not wholly within the Park, in keeping with the already surveyed E & N land grant. Then in later years, when forestry companies purchased the E & N lands and began harvesting timber on the Park's border, unsightly clear-cuts heralded visitors at the Buttle Lake entrance to the Park.

Officials in Victoria did not take into account Indigenous use of the area, neither did they consider existing timber licences and mineral claims within the new boundaries, which later resulted in some creative land-swapping arrangements with forestry companies, and the eventual development of mineral claims.

The contentious history of mining in Strathcona Park goes back to the time of the Park's formation. The original Strathcona Park Act, for example, "neither prohibited nor permitted land to be used for industrial purposes." Gold and copper continued to be mined at Big Interior Mountain after the Park's creation. The Bedwell Valley, an area of stunning lakes and rivers, was brought within Park boundaries by 1913; however, contained within the valley were active placer gold-mining operations and mineral leases. The government attempted to purchase these leases, but was unable to reach an agreement with leaseholders.

Since mining was not permitted under the original Strathcona Park Act, to get around this issue the Act was amended in 1918 to allow for limited mineral exploration, thus appeasing prospectors.[3]

Other natural resources, aside from minerals, would draw speculators to the region in this same era. Mike King, a prospector,

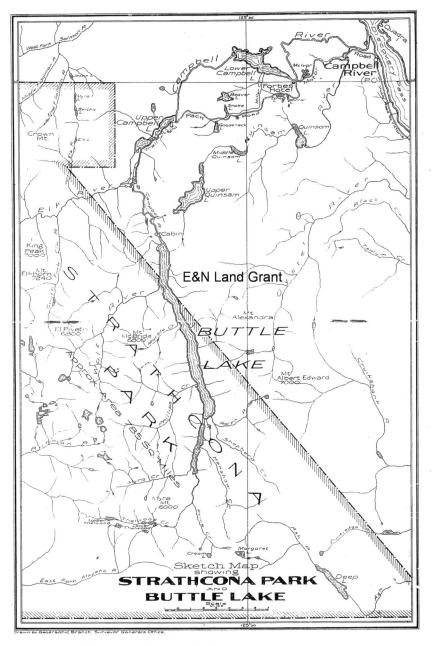

1916 Map of Strathcona Provincial Park. THE LEGISLATIVE LIBRARY OF BRITISH
COLUMBIA 1916

timber cruiser and explorer from the United States, had his eye on the region for hydro-electric development. He was known to traverse Vancouver Island on foot from Campbell River to the west coast, crossing through the Strathcona region on more than one occasion.[4] King recognized that the source of the watershed was Buttle Lake, which fed the Campbell River system, passing through Upper Campbell Lake and Lower Campbell Lake, until the river tumbled over magnificent Elk Falls before reaching the sea; in all a distance of roughly 105 kilometres.[5]

Mike King did not live to realize his dream of harnessing hydro-electric power on the Campbell River watershed, but others would show an interest. The Park Act was amended once again in 1927 to allow water levels to rise within the Park to pave the way for hydro-electric power development; however nothing went ahead at that time. These changes, and a drift toward policies favouring development of resource-rich British Columbia, meant that the history of Strathcona Park would become a history of exploitation.

The 1930s to the '60s were pivotal decades in opening the Park to industry. Those who would be most closely affected had mineral claims within the Park on which they had erected cabins, or lived in nearby Campbell River, the Comox Valley and at a wilderness lodge, Strathcona Park Lodge and Outdoor Education Centre, that has been the Park's closest neighbour since 1959. The prevailing philosophy of multiple use of park land in British Columbia was in keeping with the times and was reflected in other provincial parks such as Ontario's Algonquin Park, and in national parks such as Banff. Yet conservationists of the 1950s in BC were concerned about how hydro-electric power generation and mining would affect both Strathcona's wilderness and its waterways. One of the most renowned of these conservationists was Roderick Haig-Brown, who spoke out against allowing placer mining, hydro-electric development, logging and open-pit mining in the Park. Haig-Brown's objections to the proposal to dam Buttle Lake, which resulted in the famous "Battle for Buttle," underscore the differing values that his own community of Campbell River had about resource use and development within a park.

A significant obstacle to developing the Park as a tourist destination was that until the late 1950s, it was challenging for visitors to access the Park by automobile. Forestry companies had opened up much of the area with logging roads, but they were not suitable for the average car. Local council lobbied for the improvement of these roads west from Campbell River and asked for completion of a road to the Buttle Lake entrance of the Park. When the road was finally completed and improved upon, so that the public could easily drive from Campbell River to Buttle Lake, then down the east side of Buttle Lake to its southern end, it was not the Department of Public Works that financed the projects. Instead, the BC Power Commission built sections of the road in 1951 and 1958, followed by Western Mines Ltd., which in 1965 completed the road, illustrating the provincial government's waning interest in tourism and growing interest in opening up the Park to industry.

The 1960s, '70s and '80s were decades of conflict, when differing opinions were heard on resource development. On one hand, conservationists feared that allowing industry to access the Park's natural resources could wreak irreversible damage on a once pristine environment, while at the same time others declared that industry created jobs and directly benefited the local economy. Placer miner and author Walter Guppy, who had holdings in the Bedwell Valley dating back to the 1930s, supported Western Mines Ltd.'s plans to develop a large ore-extracting mine at Buttle Lake, made possible by Park policy altered in the early '60s to allow for significant commercial development that would include both industry and tourism. Guppy's was among the voices that spoke out in favour of industrial growth, countering those who feared that mining would destroy the Park's value for recreationists. He contended that "if important mines are developed, these will be points of interest," citing Barkerville as an example. Guppy, unlike early Park visionaries, had little appreciation of the tourism potential of Strathcona Park. He felt that most tourists would not want to "make an extended safari" into the wilderness in order to access Strathcona, which was essentially devoid of park infrastructure. "Parks that attract tourists are places where there are picnic tables and garbage cans," he maintained, writing that Park founders' notions of setting aside the Park for visitorship and recreation "was based on the misconception that the mountainous interior of Vancouver Island had recreational possibilities."[6]

Mountaineers who later became fascinated with the Park disproved Guppy's view regarding the mountainous interior and have written lyrically about the pristine beauty of the Park and the exceptional climbing opportunities afforded by its mountains.

Authors such as Lindsay Elms, Philip Stone and Rob Wood were all introduced to Strathcona Park when they came to work at Strathcona Park Lodge and Outdoor Education Centre as instructors: Wood in 1977, and Elms and Stone in the 1990s. They have all favourably compared the mountains of Strathcona Park with some of the best climbs in the world.

Wood became embroiled in environmental battles in the late 1980s, when provincial policy withdrew protection from pristine areas known to mountaineers, specifically Cream Lake. He helped form the Friends of Strathcona Park, a group that took a militant approach to protesting the proposed changes that would allow for a second mine in the Park at Cream Lake, with their actions ultimately leading to civil disobedience.

Finally, the Ministry of the Environment put in place long-term policies that would protect the wilderness values of the Park, described in its 1993 Master Plan for Strathcona Park. Two years later, the Strathcona Wilderness Institute emerged to continue supporting the objectives of the Friends of Strathcona Park and to work with BC Parks providing education and information for students and park visitors, taking the place of the interpretation programs first developed by BC Parks. Parks administration experienced numerous changes in the century since Strathcona Park was formed, and today, certain Park functions are contracted out to companies that supervise campgrounds and maintenance. Overall,

BC Parks plays a strong role in coordination with current industry in the Park and in decision making for the present and future use of Strathcona Park.

As more of the public discovers the attractions of this outstanding wilderness area, it is hoped visitors will take the time to acquaint themselves with its history and its sensitivity and will understand and appreciate the effort made to protect this area for recreationists.

GOING BACK TO WHERE IT ALL BEGAN

Signs of elk are seen at places, notably on the North Fork of Elk River. Deer are plentiful. Black bear are frequently seen. Panther are not often seen, except if systematically hunted, but are evidently numerous. There are some wolves. Their howling can be heard at times across the lakes. Beaver are plentiful in most of the valleys, particularly at head-waters of the Gold River. There are also otter and marten. Of feathered game, the grouse is found everywhere, the blue grouse being found on the hillsides and timbered ridges and willow-grouse in the valleys. Duck of all varieties and geese abound during the migratory seasons and a few remain during the summer to breed. The loon is much in evidence at all times. Trout abound in all lakes and streams without exception.

STRATHCONA PARK, VANCOUVER ISLAND
pamphlet from the BC Department of Lands, 1921

THE IMPULSE TO set aside areas as park land in North America began in the United States in the early 1800s, when certain visionaries recognized that some of the country's wilderness should remain untouched by development and settlement. To protect hot springs located in Arkansas, Hot Springs Reservation was created in 1832; then in 1864, the Yosemite Valley and Mariposa Grove of Giant Sequoias were set aside in California, and later in 1899, Yosemite achieved national park status. Yellowstone National Park was created in 1872 to protect its lands from private ownership and to ensure that the wildlife, geysers and waterfalls would remain untouched for the enjoyment of the public. The creation of parks did not always occur without opposition, and some felt these areas should be open to logging concerns. Companies that provided hydro-electric power in some cases expected to be able to build dam projects within parks boundaries.[1] This multiple-use idea would also plague Canadian parks, particularly provincial parks, and confusion would arise as to the meaning of conservation since industrialists would claim that conservation meant using land for its highest and best use in the interest of the public, even if that conflicted with retaining land in its natural state. Those who wished to protect park resources from any industrial exploitation were labelled "preservationists."

In Canada, Rocky Mountains Park was established in Alberta in 1885 at the location of a hot springs that was also along a Canadian Pacific Railway (CPR) line, and was later renamed Banff National

Chateau Lake Louise. MYRNA BOULDING COLLECTION

Park. Rail lines made for easy access to Banff and other stunning areas for those who had the leisure and wealth to afford it. In 1886, Glacier and Yoho National Parks were created in British Columbia, and in all parks, hotels such as Banff Springs Hotel and Chateau Lake Louise were constructed to provide both food and lodging for train travellers. This allowed the CPR to discontinue the onerous practice of hauling its heavy dining cars through steep mountain passes.[2]

The region had no settlements or Indigenous villages; Indigenous people however, were accustomed to hunting within the park's boundaries. Their presence and practices were perceived to conflict with tourist use, and in 1887, shortly after Banff National Park was created, Indigenous people were forbidden to hunt in the park. This practice was repeated in other provinces. Hunting was prohibited in Ontario in 1893 within the new "Algonquin National Park" north of Toronto, which was later renamed Algonquin Provincial Park. In Quebec, when "Laurentides National Park," which became Parc national du Mont-Tremblant, was created in January of 1895, similar legislation was applied. At the municipal level, Indigenous people and any others residing in Stanley Park in Vancouver were evicted.[3]

The region that comprises Strathcona Provincial Park was considered to be Crown land and had no settlements within the boundaries set aside as reserve land; however, the decision to select this territory was made in Victoria, far to the south, without any consultation with nearby First Nations regarding their use of the area. In the European view, if people did not inhabit a certain territory, then they were not exhibiting any signs of ownership. When Captain George Vancouver sailed the British Columbia coast in 1792, he observed uninhabited Indigenous villages and assumed they were abandoned, not realizing that they were used on a seasonal basis.

The earliest inhabitants of Vancouver Island are considered to have come across the Bering Land Bridge when water levels were low, about 15,000 years ago, or to have arrived by water, approaching from the northwest.[4] Some theorists believe coastal people of British Columbia are related to Polynesians. Many First Nations have origin stories that place them in the Vancouver Island region from the beginning of time, and these sacred places are home, are the beginning.

Although we don't know how long people have inhabited the region, recent archaeological finds keep pushing the date further back into the past. In terms of geology, some areas of coastal British Columbia escaped the last Ice Age and First Nations villages survived. On Triquet Island, located on BC's central coast about 150 kilometres north of Port Hardy, a village site uncovered in 2017 is believed to be about 14,000 years old.[5]

Recent studies on sea levels are revealing that historical levels are much different than previously believed, and that today's levels are roughly 192 metres above what they were 14,000 years ago. A 2018 study concluded that freshwater lakes which exist today on places such as Quadra Island were likely tidal flats, or salt water, during the last Ice Age.[6]

New finds along the Campbell River watershed support these conclusions. At Lower Campbell and Upper Campbell Lakes, which may have at one time been inlets, artifacts such as arrowheads have been found by archaeologists. BC Hydro is supporting these studies, recognizing that at the time the Campbell River watershed was flooded to support hydro-electric projects, archaeology was not taken into consideration. Owen Grant of Baseline Archaeology is heading up the project.

Grant has explained that within Park boundaries at Buttle Lake, where water levels have not changed drastically since the three dams along the watershed were constructed, archaeologists in 2019 uncovered over fifty sites that contained evidence of tool making, with over 1,000 artifacts uncovered that are at this writing still being catalogued. Since these finds are new, exact dating has not been confirmed, but preliminary estimates are that the sites date back several thousand years, and further research will determine if they extend back 14,000 years, the date of the Triquet Island site.

A quarry site and butchering site at Buttle Lake point to stone tool making and artifacts related to hunting such as projectile points and arrow points that would perhaps be left in a carcass, as well as microblade cores that remain after the blades are flaked off the stone. The most common stone found quarried is green flint-like chert, but, surprisingly, an obsidian stone was also found, which does not occur on Vancouver Island.[7]

Anthropologists and archaeologists had supposed that humans of this region inhabited only the coast and river estuaries going back about 2,500 to 5,000 years. It is thought the Mowachaht of Nootka Island, for example, have been on the coast for about 4,000 years. With the realization that lakes such as Buttle were probably tidal flats and occupied, ideas of the prehistory and the whole pattern of settlement for this region and the region that comprises Strathcona Park have changed drastically. In light of these finds, estimates are that archaeological work will carry on into 2030.

"The archaeology," said Jesse Morin, who worked at the sites, "will tell the whole story."[8]

Strathcona Park has special features: the Park contains the largest stands of old growth of any coastal park, and the tallest Douglas firs in Canada, as well as rare plant species. It is the only park on the Pacific Coast south of Alaska with a completely virgin

A snarling cougar, photo taken by Joe Drinkwater, circa 1920. IMAGE PN12039
ALBERNI VALLEY MUSEUM PHOTOGRAPH COLLECTION

watershed to the sea. Within Park boundaries is Della Falls, one of the highest waterfalls in North America, and the Golden Hinde, Vancouver Island's highest mountain.[9]

The natural history of Vancouver Island and the Park is unique, with distinct geology not related to the province's mainland. Philip Stone in *Exploring Strathcona Park* has commented that "Vancouver Island, which sits on its own mini continental plate, once resided alongside the islands of the Indonesian archipelago."[10]

Unique mammals found on Vancouver Island provide a good example of the Island's alienation from the mainland, represented by the presence of Roosevelt elk and Vancouver Island marmots, and the curious absence of grizzly bears (unless they swim over), moose, foxes, coyotes, skunks, badgers, chipmunks or porcupines. Black bears are common, as are wolves, cougars, black-tailed deer and pine martens, mink and numerous deer mice.

Researchers say it is difficult to link ancient archaeological finds with more recent Indigenous presence on Vancouver Island, but there is evidence of both ancient and more contemporary hunting of the same mammals. It is certain that the Muchalaht People, who occupied the Muchalat Inlet to the west of today's Park near present day Gold River from about 4,000 years ago up until the early 1900s, went into the Island's interior to hunt and pick berries. Elk would have been a welcome addition to the diet of peoples who normally consumed salmon and shellfish, and elk hides offer warmth, while the bones can be used to make tools.

Evidence of marmot hunting by Nuu-chah-nulth Peoples of the Northwest Coast is relatively recent, with finds beginning in 1985. The Vancouver Island marmot (*Marmota vancouverensis*), now an endangered species, is a "burrowing, colonial rodent that inhabits alpine and subalpine areas in the Mountain Hemlock and Alpine biogeoclimatic zones."[11] In 1992, Marlene and Steve Smith found a cave on the east side of Mariner Mountain and, going inside, were surprised to encounter a pile of bones. Upon closer inspection, they realized they probably were looking at marmot remains, and due to the number of bones and marks present on them, particularly the skulls, they believed the marmots must have been killed by human hands. A 1996 study published by David W. Nagorsen, Grant Keddie and Tanya Luszcz reveals numerous intriguing conclusions: that marmots were skinned and butchered for meat, that Indigenous Peoples travelled to remote mountain areas to hunt marmots and that this hunting occurred roughly 800 to 2,600 years ago. At the Mariner site alone, 1,937 bone specimens representing marmot, black-tailed deer, black bear and marten were collected in the cave; single fish and bird bones were also found, along with three artifacts comprised of "a California mussel (*Mytilus californianus*) shell which could be a knife fragment,... a flaked stone with a naturally sharp edge,... probably used for skinning, and... an abrading or sharpening stone most likely used to sharpen tools. A piece of burned wood was also collected on the cave floor."[12] Specimens were also found at the Golden Hinde in Strathcona Park. It is hoped that the finds may help explain why the population of marmots, which were once plentiful throughout the Park region but which are no longer present in the cave areas, has declined.

Salish Peoples such as the Pentlatch, who occupied the east coast of Vancouver Island and outlying islands for centuries, would likewise have made forays into the interior of Vancouver Island to hunt and gather, as did the Kwakwa̱ka'wakw (Laich-Kwil-Tach) of present day Campbell River.[13] Nuu-chah-nulth Peoples to the southwest and south of the Park, such as the Ahousaht, Tla-o-qui-aht, Tseshaht and Hupacasath, would most certainly have used this region, not only for hunting but also, like the other groups, for spiritual purposes. Certain stories related to spirit quests and transformations are linked to tall mountains and waterfalls such as those found in the Park. This is corroborated by evidence gathered by Mowachaht/Muchalaht First Nation (MMFN) research:

> Ritual preparation sites, generally found at higher elevations, or at caves, lakes, waterfalls and other features, are considered private knowledge and are owned by specific families. There are also traditional histories associated with some areas in the park.

Trails existed through the present day Park, such as a Gold River to Alberni trail, used by the Opetchesaht (Hupacasath) People to attack the Muchalaht during the Mowachaht/Muchalaht war, which took place around 1850.[14] A reluctance on the part of K'omoks/Pentlatch People to enter the interior of the Island can be traced back to their fear of the Alberni nations.

Most trails were considered trading trails in times of peace. A well-established trading trail existed between Tahsis and the Nimpkish region farther north, used by the Mowachaht and Nimpkish Peoples, and

> a network of trails and canoe routes ran through what is now the Strathcona Park, and followed a series of known campsites. These trails were used as trading routes and for visiting neighbours. Muchalaht people travelled along a trail system that

followed what are now called the Gold, Heber and Elk River systems and eventually led to the Campbell River area.[15]

The present highway (28) to Gold River is based upon the Gold River to Campbell River trail, and a prospector by the name of Harry Linberg described this trail in his testimony to an inquisition that took place related to a questionable death in 1932, demonstrating that locally it was both known and used at that time. In his deposition he wrote:

> I went down that day to the Government Ferry that is another ten miles on the main Campbell River trail going from Campbell Lake by the Nootka trail right across the island. Before I got four miles I had to go through the brush to Parama River. I spent that night in an Indian shack their smoke house there were blankets there and dishes.[16]

He went on to describe accessing the Campbell River trail, travelling for five or six miles, but was unable to cross a river as the foot bridge was washed out. He travelled along the river until he was able find the trail that took him to Drum Lake, where he came across a trapper's cabin, then went on to stay at a government cabin that had been built by surveyors at Lady Falls. After a night at the cabin, he mentioned having to cross a river, perhaps the Elk River, where the trail became indistinct.

After this crossing he reached the Sutherland brothers' trapper's cabin, where he spent the night. The next morning he reached the end of the trail at a river but had been told to expect it to end at a lake. Devising a raft, he made it to Upper Campbell Lake, crossed it and landed. Here he found another cabin he surmised belonged to the Sutherlands. He hiked down to the eastern end of the lake and found the Sutherland provisioning camp, where the men who were present helped him procure a ride by automobile into Campbell River.

This [trail] was linked with another travel route that went down the Buttle Lake and, from there, across to Comox. There were canoes left at either end of Buttle Lake for travellers to traverse the lake. Another route through the park started at the south end of Buttle Lake and went down Bedwell River to Bedwell Inlet. Another trail led from the end of Muchalaht Inlet, Matchlee Bay, up the Burman River and then across to Great Central Lake and eventually led to what is now Port Alberni. There were also smaller trails that led to resource areas (hunting, fishing, trapping, berries, bark, plants, medicinal plants and other resources) throughout many areas in the park. Unfortunately, only a few of the many indigenous place names for rivers, mountains, lakes and other features were recorded in the past, or have been passed down and are remembered today.[17]

Natural History

The waterways were an important component of these travel routes, and the drainage systems originating in Strathcona Park from higher elevations all naturally lead to the sea. Early explorers would take advantage of these water routes to access the interior of the Island, and today it is recognized that not only are the watersheds vital to freshwater ecosystems, but also to salmon. Salmon, inhibited by waterfalls, do not migrate into the upper reaches of the Park, but their health is closely linked to that of the interior streams and lakes. Cutthroat, rainbow and Dolly Varden trout can be fished at Buttle Lake, particularly at the mouths of creeks and rivers.

Major drainage systems to the west coast include Bedwell River from Bedwell Lake; Burman River from Bancroft Creek; Gold River from the Ucona River, Gold and Donner Lakes; Megin River from Watta Creek and Mitla Creek; the Moyeha River from Abco, Mariner and Kowus Creeks; the Somass River (via Stamp River and Great Central Lake) to the Ash River, Oshinow Lake and Drinkwater Creek.

To the east coast in the Forbidden Plateau region are Brown's River from Paradise and Wattaway Creeks, McKenzie, Lady, Croteau and Battleship Lakes; Gem Lake and Lake Helen MacKenzie; and the Puntledge River from the Cruickshank River and Rees, Eric and Comox Lakes.

Farther north, the Oyster River, Piggot, Norm, Gem and Harris Creeks, Memory and Moat Lakes are all along the same system, and from the Buttle Lake region, the Elk, Ralph and Wolf Rivers, and the Cervus, Tlools, Myra and Thelwood Creeks all feed Buttle Lake, which then flows into Campbell River via the Upper and Lower Campbell Lakes and the John Hart Reservoir. The Salmon River in the Sayward District is fed by Crowned Creek.[18]

The Park's waters support waterfowl as well as fish; ducks such as the green-winged teal, hooded mergansers and buffleheads can be spotted, as well as Canada geese, blue herons and kingfishers. Trumpeter swans winter in the shallows of Buttle Narrows.

Strathcona Park is unique in that it contains life zones ranging from sea level to alpine heights. The cold, snowy, windswept area above the tree line over 1,675 metres elevation is the Alpine Zone and Coastal Alpine Tundra Subzone; in the lower Mountain Hemlock Zone and Maritime Forested and Parkland Subzone at about 1,200 metres, amabilis fir and yellow-cedar are found, dependent on unfrozen ground beneath the snow. Hikers are rewarded with a plethora of alpine wildflowers appearing in varied hues.

The Maritime Forested Subzone is characterized by gnarled mountain hemlock and continuity of forest cover, as well as dense vegetation in the form of highbush blueberry and huckleberry.[19]

One of the more interesting aspects of Strathcona Park geology is the presence of limestone, fossils, karst formations and caves. The Karst Creek trail at Buttle Lake offers a close look at karst in action: the eroding limestone creates underground caverns into which streams will disappear, only to reappear farther along. Ancient relatives of the starfish are found in white limestone near the waterfall.[20]

The most predominant rock type found in Strathcona Park is volcanic basalt, and the Park's highest peaks, such as Mt Albert Edward, the Golden Hinde, Castlecrag, Mt Alexandra, Jutland, Mt Septimus and Mt Colonel Foster, with their lava formations, are made up of this rock. In addition, their present appearance indicates to geologists that these peaks were perhaps not covered during the last period of glaciation. "Deglaciation," according to naturalist Betty Brooks, "began 14,000 years ago, and the ice probably had receded to its present limits as recently as 8,000 years ago."[21] Numerous glaciers or remnant ice caps occur on north facing slopes sheltered from the sun at the highest elevations in the Park and are found on Mariner Mountain, Mt Tom Taylor, Big Interior Mountain, Nine Peaks, Mt Myra and the Comox Glacier complex, the Golden Hinde and the Elkhorn.[22]

Early Explorers

Much of the Park is rich in minerals. Whether late nineteenth-century explorers knew this or not, when Commander John Buttle headed a government sponsored Vancouver Island Exploring Expedition into the region in 1865, he instructed other members of his party to be on the lookout for gold in the streams they encountered. Buttle Lake derives its name from Buttle, who described a lake with islands situated between mountains and about twenty miles in length. It has been postulated, though, that Buttle was in fact looking at Great Central Lake, since from his vantage point he would not have been able to see as far north as Buttle Lake.[23] Buttle's opportunity to lead this expedition came when Dr. Robert Brown, who headed up the Vancouver Island Exploring Expedition and survey of 1864 into the south central interior region of Vancouver Island, recommended him. Buttle had accompanied Brown on this earlier foray into the interior as a botanist.

The party began at Clayoquot Sound on Vancouver Island's west coast on Buttle's recommendation, and indeed, precious minerals were discovered by a member and miner in Buttle's party, Magin Hancock. Hancock found gold at Bear River, today's Bedwell River. According to Walter Guppy, "within two weeks there were over one hundred men prospecting the area,"[24] many of them idle prospectors from Victoria still hopeful of finding riches in British Columbia. As it happened, few made significant discoveries and only a group of Chinese miners stayed on into the 1880s before giving up.

Again the search for minerals would figure largely in the 1896 adventures of Reverend William W. Bolton, who specified that he hoped "to discover gold and copper in this new world."[25] Originally from England and a headmaster of Victoria's University for Boys, Bolton organized a party with the objective of completing an earlier trip he had made to explore the north central section of the Island.

The explorers travelled by steamer from Victoria along the east side of Vancouver Island and reached Alert Bay on Cormorant Island July 3. From here they crossed the strait by canoe to the mouth of the Nimpkish River on Vancouver Island. They made it to Woss Lake, then possibly followed the long established trade route or "grease trail" of the Nimpkish and west coast Mowachaht Peoples that ended at the head of the Tahsis Inlet.

They travelled by water down the inlet to Gold River where supplies were waiting, took some photographs of the Muchalaht People and their dwellings, and looked for a way to Buttle Lake from there. It seems they were unaware of established trails and forded their own challenging way across, but did realize that by following the Wolf River, at that time called the Mosquito, they would find Buttle Lake. After reaching the lake, they met a supply party waiting for them on the Campbell River. Now they were ready for the last leg of their journey, up and over the divide from Buttle Lake to Great Central Lake, which they reached ahead of schedule. Although they did not find minerals on their journey, they did travel from one end of Vancouver Island to the other, took photographs of contemporary scenes and Indigenous people on their way, and created a map of

A Muchalaht village in the late 1800s. IMAGE CR015013 COURTESY OF THE
MUSEUM AT CAMPBELL RIVER ARCHIVES

their explorations. Mountaineer and local historian Lindsay Elms
noted that "Bolton was most meticulous in keeping a journal of the
trips and these provide a fascinating description of life on the trail
as well as a description of isolated settlements and native villages at
the close of the nineteenth century."[26]

Mineral exploration continued, although the next significant
discovery after Hancock's was accidental. In 1899, Joe Drinkwater, an outdoorsman, trapper and prospector, set out to prove,
based on a bet, that it was possible to hike from Bedwell Sound
to Alberni. Following the trail made by the earlier prospectors
along the Bear (Bedwell) River, once he reached a fork in the valley, Drinkwater then travelled in an easterly direction alongside
You Creek. He reached Big Interior Mountain and near the summit
observed a green hue in the rock, indicating the presence of copper, and staked a claim. Further exploration in the area took him
to a beautiful lake nestled in a valley between Nine Peaks and Big
Interior Mountain. Here he found gold and staked another claim.
While there, he became aware of the sound of cascading water, and
at the outlet of the lake observed an outstanding series of three

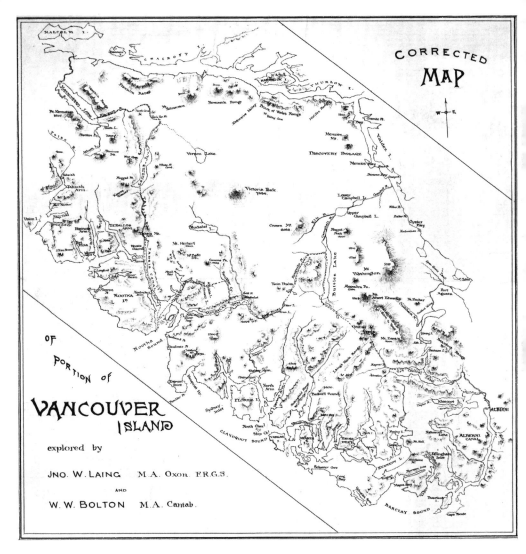

waterfalls, 1,440 feet in height, that dropped into a canyon below. He lowered himself down the rock face alongside the falls and eventually reached a basin where the falls flowed into a creek that later became known as Drinkwater Creek. Following the creek, he found himself at Great Central Lake. The rest of the journey was by water across the lake to reach Alberni.

Drinkwater returned to develop his gold claim at the lake, which he named Della in honour of his wife. The magnificent waterfalls became known as Della Falls.[27]

OPPOSITE William Bolton's map of the region he explored in 1896 showing many features of the Park already named. IMAGE CM/A914 COURTESY OF THE ROYAL BC MUSEUM AND ARCHIVES

ABOVE, LEFT Trapper Joe Drinkwater with his cougar prize. IMAGE PN13229 ALBERNI VALLEY MUSEUM PHOTOGRAPH COLLECTION

ABOVE, RIGHT The magnificent Della Falls. IMAGE PN03729 ALBERNI VALLEY MUSEUM PHOTOGRAPH COLLECTION

Seven miles of roads were built from Great Central Lake to gain access to the Drinkwater copper mine site called the Ptarmigan Mine, but the advent of war in 1914 discouraged any further work. Walter Guppy asserts, however, that the most inhibiting factor to mining was the founding of Strathcona Park in 1911.[28]

There were other natural resources aside from minerals that would draw speculators to the region in this era. Mike King, a prospector, timber cruiser and explorer from the United States, who had been logging in the Comox Valley and Campbell River

ABOVE The Drinkwater mine at Big Interior Mountain. IMAGE PN00264 ALBERNI VALLEY MUSEUM PHOTOGRAPH COLLECTION

OPPOSITE Mike King. IMAGE B-03726 COURTESY OF THE ROYAL BC MUSEUM AND ARCHIVES

areas, had his eye on the region for hydro-electric development. King was described as

> an indefatigable worker, a shrewd though generous business man, and one of the most expert timber cruisers in the northwest, Mr. King was a prince of entertainers. He was fond of stories of personal experiences, many of which were demonstrations of the truth of the adage that truth is stranger than fiction. Naturally, in his wanderings in British Columbia, he had come in personal touch with the Indians, was able to discourse fluently in their Patois, and his intimate knowledge of their character enabled him to pilot himself safely through many a tight corner. His favorite exclamation: "By the Lovely Dove" is passport to the good fellowship of foresters from Mexico to Alaska.[29]

Michael King and his brother James came to the Campbell River and Comox Valley districts with their partner Lewis Casey from the northwestern United States in the 1880s, although Mike King made a home in Victoria. They acquired 360 acres along the

Campbell River that they planned to log, as well as land at Duncan Bay, three miles north of Campbell River, where they had plans to develop a townsite around the natural, deep water harbour.[30]

For several years, the intrepid trio explored much of Vancouver Island on foot, all the while considering potential of the timber, mineral and water resources they took note of. Mike King often went alone or in the company of local Indigenous guides. While at Lower Campbell Lake, he saw an island he "gave" to his wife Mary, now underwater.[31]

King had property in the Comox Valley where he stabled the oxen used in his logging operations. His favourite place to stay while in Comox was at the Lorne Hotel, owned and operated by Samuel and Florence Cliffe. On one occasion in 1892, he described to the Cliffes "a beautiful creek with falls near where it tumbled into Buttle Lake, and also a mountain nearby," which he had seen on one of his numerous excursions through that region, and pulling Myra, the Cliffes' five-year-old daughter, upon his knee, "he asked Mrs. Cliffe if he could call his discoveries after the little girl." The names, however, did not immediately appear on maps of the Strathcona region.[32]

Familiar with the watershed that originated at Buttle Lake and flowed through lakes and the river until the Campbell River tumbled over magnificent Elk Falls before reaching the sea—in all a distance of roughly sixty miles to the coast at Campbell River— King was well aware of its hydro-electric potential.[33] Claude Harrison in 1926 confirmed that King felt Elk Falls alone could produce about 100,000 horsepower (HP), but "with a possible development of a further 50,000 or 75,000 HP, fed by a chain of lakes comprising Buttle Lake in Strathcona Park, then Upper Campbell Lake, then Campbell Lake itself—each with an enormous watershed."[34] In 1909 King engaged Harrison to stake the falls and put up notices, a requirement that would ensure proprietorship, and Harrison managed to do so, just hours ahead of a large corporation intent on doing the same. As a result of his efforts, the water rights were granted to King.

King had now taken the first important step in the development of his vision of a hydro-electric project, but he did not live to see it to fruition. He died of injuries received on a trip he took across the Island from the west coast to the east coast in the spring of 1910.

King had boarded a steamer in Victoria that he took north to the coast in the Nootka Sound area, with the intent of looking over a property he had that contained coal. The steamer was unable to retrieve him for a return trip due to stormy weather, so King, as he had many times before, set out on foot to cross Vancouver Island along the familiar trail from the Gold River region to Campbell River. From here, he could catch another steamer back to Victoria. An account in the *Daily Colonist* describes the incident that would eventually lead to his passing:

The Fatal Accident

En route [across the Island] Mr. King slipped while walking a moss-covered log and fell some thirty feet down a rocky cliff. He sustained serious injuries. His ankle was twisted and there was a pain in his side besides bruises. The woodsman brushed aside the incident as a mere trifle. Picking himself up he limped over miles of the roughest kind of trail to Buttle lake.

While attempting to construct a rude raft in order to cross the lake, Mr. King was found by "Lord" Bacon, a trapper who was operating in the vicinity. Mr. Bacon placed the injured man in his canoe and paddled to the lower end of the lake, and then down the turbulent Upper Campbell river to a lodge occupied at times by the trapper.

"He was in a sorry plight when he reached my cabin," said Bacon. "He was hungry, lame and ill; his clothes were torn his gun was bent and broken; and altogether he presented a very melancholy appearance.

"I tried to get him to stay in my cabin for a few days until I could get help to take him out. This he refused, saying that he was feeling fine and could easily do the remaining thirty miles to the settlement; so, packing a bit of lunch in his handkerchief and using his heavy, but useless rifle as a cane the poor old fellow hobbled out in the brush alone and made for home.

"The man was certainly in no condition to be in the woods at all, and had it been anybody in the country except 'Mike' King, whose strength, courage and woodcraft were so well known to me, I would never have trusted him outside the door."[35]

The man at Buttle Lake who gave him a hand, Bacon, and who referred to himself as "Lord," was to figure prominently in a government sponsored expedition formed later that year to explore the Buttle Lake region, in consideration of its suitability as park land.[36]

Mike King died of his injuries at Victoria's Jubilee Hospital at the age of sixty-two on December 18, 1910. In the obituary for King published in the *Colonist*, he was said to be "A typical westerner, possessing a passion for the wilds, business acumen which enabled him to turn to commercial advantage the knowledge he secured in his travels and a heart as expansive as the territory he roamed,... King was loved by his intimate friends and held in the highest esteem by his acquaintances."[37]

King's failure to realize his dream was one of many doomed schemes to come. Helen Mitchell noted in 1966 that "the struggle for the rights to the enormous hydro-electric potentialities of the Campbell River began more than 60 years ago, and the issue was raised and allowed to fall into obscurity several times, for more than 40 years, before the river was eventually harnessed."[38]

WHY ARE THERE NO ROADS INTO THE PARK?

There is no road at present into the Park. Motors can travel to within a mile of Upper Campbell Lake, or about 12 miles beyond Forbes Landing, but there is no accommodation to store cars beyond that place. From the end of the road a trail follows along the southerly side of Campbell Lake and the east side of Campbell River to Buttle Lake.

STRATHCONA PARK, VANCOUVER ISLAND
pamphlet from the BC Department of Lands, 1921

W HEN GROUPS IN Victoria such as the Natural History Society of British Columbia, the Victoria Board of Trade, the Tourist Association of Victoria and the Vancouver Island Development League began lobbying the provincial government to establish a park on Vancouver Island, Premier Richard McBride (1903–1915) took their petitions into consideration and began looking for suitable acreage. Initially, Cameron Lake, in the central part of the island beside today's MacMillan Park (Cathedral Grove) and fifteen kilometres east of Alberni, was considered as a reserve. A road already existed to the community of Alberni from Nanaimo, and in Nanaimo there was a rail line to Victoria. However Cameron Lake was not on Crown land; it was encompassed within the original Esquimalt and Nanaimo land grant, portions of which had been sold to private timber interests by that time. Due to these timber rights, the provincial government was not able to secure the area as park land.

Looking farther north, McBride considered the region explored by Bolton several years earlier, his imagination no doubt stimulated by Bolton's poetic account of Buttle Lake, written in Bolton's diary on August 5, 1896:

> It is, so far as the writer's knowledge extends, the peer of all the island lakes in its scenic beauty. Banked on both sides by high mountains, snow-capped and rugged, there is a lower range still closer to it covered in most parts to the water's edge with fair

sized timber. Numerous waterfalls pour down on either side of the lake, and streams, some large but mostly small, are in plenty. At the little beaches where we rested we saw plenty of evidence that deer abound. We camped just inside the timber at the head of the lake and the view from this spot is one that would entrance an artist.[1]

McBride set aside 174,000 hectares on June 2, 1910, as a reserve, and a year later expanded this area to 215,000 hectares.[2]

The Byronesque wistfulness in Bolton's account was to be repeated by later authors describing in lyrical terms the region's scenery. Vancouver Island was Canada's last western frontier. Although Fort Victoria on its southern tip, built in 1843, was the first community in what was to become British Columbia and on Vancouver Island, the Island's unknown interior remained a mystery.

In the late nineteenth century, the world was becoming global, and at the close of the century, Britain occupied one-fifth of it. Even though Canada achieved Dominion status in 1867 with Confederation, Britain's influence in the fledgling nation remained strong both politically and culturally. Britain had been preoccupied for three and a half centuries with consolidating its vast empire beginning with expeditions sanctioned by the first Queen Elizabeth, and to that end the island nation financed countless expeditions around the globe. This fervour to be the first and the strongest did not die with the end of the nineteenth century, but carried on into the twentieth.

At the start of the new century, British explorers were engaged in the race to reach the earth's two poles. Just as thoughts were turning to plan for a park on Vancouver Island, instead of the British, two Americans, Robert Peary in 1909 and Frederick Albert Cook in 1908, claimed to have reached the geographic north pole. Roald Amundsen of Norway arrived at the south pole on December 14, 1911, just five weeks ahead of the British explorer Robert Scott. The age of great explorations was coming to an end. New horizons

ABOVE, LEFT Buttle Lake. WILL J. REID FAMILY COLLECTION

ABOVE, RIGHT Myra Falls. WILL J. REID FAMILY COLLECTION

and new challenges were limited as the entire world became mapped and surveyed, with one of the few uncharted territories at the beginning of the twentieth century being the unknown lands between northern India and Tibet. The subsequent survey by the British led to the "discovery" of Mt Everest, and a new pinnacle to conquer.

The world in the nineteenth century experienced unprecedented growth and change characterized by the Industrial Revolution, which in many areas created a blight on the landscape, pollution and noise from factories. In fact, the results of industrializing and the increasing pace of modern life encouraged many to long for a past represented by Arcadia.

The unspoiled beauty of the interior of Vancouver Island appealed to those who already felt overwhelmed by western development. Although industrialization came later to Canada than it did to Europe, it was rapidly spreading across the country from east to west in the late nineteenth century. On November 7, 1885, the last spike in the Canadian Pacific rail line, that joined east with west, was driven home by Donald Smith, Lord Strathcona, whose name would be chosen twenty-six years later for Vancouver Island's largest park. Now that trains could begin bringing passengers by the hundreds to Canada's westernmost province, the west would no longer be an unspoiled, uncharted frontier, and Vancouver, as the western terminus, would experience dramatic growth. Long sea voyages around Cape Horn, the southern tip of South America, or arduous land journeys by wagon or horse did not need to be undertaken in order to reach the west coast of Canada.

The rail terminus was initially supposed to have been on Vancouver Island; however earlier attempts to bring the rail lines over to the Island failed when surveys of Bute Inlet proved how onerous and expensive the task would be. Victoria missed out on being the "end of the line," and ten years after the 1858 Fraser Canyon gold rush was over and prospectors left, the population dwindled dramatically from several hundred thousand to just 5,000. The Colony of Vancouver Island, formed in 1849, merged with the Colony of British Columbia on the mainland in 1866, and the provincial capital moved from Victoria to New Westminster on the mainland, but returned to Victoria two years later. Then, due to efforts by pro-confederationists such as the colourful Amor de Cosmos, politician and publisher of the *British Colonist*, the entire westernmost colony joined the rest of Canada in 1871.[3]

A criteria for British Columbia to join the rest of the country included completion of the rail line to the west coast, and this in turn consolidated the commercial dream of a Dominion empire. The fur trade had first opened up the country, and the Hudson's Bay Company's (HBC) reach into the west included trade along the coast of Vancouver Island. When the fur trade proved to be no longer lucrative by the late 1800s, the HBC turned to mining. Coal brought to HBC officers by Indigenous people of the Nanaimo region stimulated an interest in the central part of the island. The Company then sold its interests to the Vancouver Coal Mining and Land Company in 1862. Scotsman Robert Dunsmuir had been a mine manager for the HBC at Nanaimo, and when the HBC left he started his own independent company, the Dunsmuir Company, and commenced operations at Wellington, where a rich coal seam had been discovered. By 1880, he had become a leading industrialist in British Columbia and owner of the Esquimalt and Nanaimo Railway. Dunsmuir was known for his brutality and tight-fistedness toward his mine employees and his extravagance during the construction of his new Victoria home, Craigdarroch Castle.[4]

Although Vancouver Island would not be connected to the rest of the country by rail, the dreams of a rail line on Vancouver Island had not died altogether, as rail transportation was a favoured mode of transportation for both passengers and freight. To that end, in 1883, the province ceded 7,689 square kilometres of land to the Dominion government to build a railroad. The Dominion in turn negotiated with Dunsmuir to build a rail line from Esquimalt to just north of Nanaimo at Wellington. Once the line reached as far as Nanaimo by 1887, a distance of 120 kilometres, the entire parcel of land was given over to the rail company. Known as the E & N (Esquimalt and Nanaimo) land grant, the amount of territory it encompassed was enormous. Even at the time, Vancouver Island residents were shocked at the stupendous size of the grant that covered approximately one quarter of Vancouver Island, and many understood the wealth it entailed. Comprising roughly two million acres, the grant included all mineral and timber wealth within its borders. The territory covered by the grant was given away with no consultation with or permissions from First Nations, just as rail lands on the mainland were expropriated by the CPR. Areas of the grant land on which settlers were residing, however, had to be forfeited by the rail company. The legacy of this transaction was to have repercussions for decades to come.[5]

In 1885, a survey of the grant was conducted by William Ralph, DLS. He drew the southern boundary of the grant from a trial line at the head of Saanich Inlet to the mouth of Muir Creek. From here, a western boundary would be drawn that went as far north as Crown Mountain, within today's Strathcona Park, that Ralph commenced work on in 1890. He referred to nautical charts of that era and based his calculations on latitude and longitude. Beginning on August 4 he set posts every half-mile as he went, and by September 19, 1892, stopping during winter, he set his last post at 135 miles. The northern boundary was to be a straight line from Crown Mountain to Seymour Narrows, just north of Campbell River; however this was later altered to match the fiftieth parallel of latitude, in the southern part of today's city of Campbell River, signalled at present by a sign on the coastal Island Highway. The eastern border of the grant was the eastern coastline of Vancouver Island from the grant's point of commencement.[6]

Shortly after acquiring the land, Dunsmuir's Esquimalt & Nanaimo Railway Company began subdividing the grant into parcels. Dunsmuir was interested in keeping mineral rights but not timber, although about twenty-five years later, in 1910, his son, James Dunsmuir, sold his coal mining interests in the granted lands for $11 million.

Private companies that purchased the timber lots, unimpeded by the province's regulations, were able to harvest the timber however they wished. This coincided with an Act of 1888 that made it easier to log on Crown land, and between 1903 and 1907, British Columbia experienced a veritable "timber rush." The timber industry of all of British Columbia was significantly aided by the 1886 completion of the Canadian Pacific Railway, opening up trade with the Prairies; then the opening of the Panama Canal in 1914 made it possible to supply international markets.[7]

In order to make up for grant land lost to already established settlers, the E & N was issued a second grant of 86,763 acres or 35,112 hectares in October 1905. That same year, the CPR purchased the E & N Railway for one million dollars and paid an additional $1.25 million for the remaining 566,580 hectares of land that had not yet been sold to other interests. Part of this parcel encompassed Forbidden Plateau, a wilderness subalpine region in the Comox Valley. The addition to the grant was surveyed in 1909 and 1910 by Colonel William J.H. Holmes, DLS, who was responsible for drawing the northern boundary. Holmes was described by Harold McClure Johnson as a "Very fine looking man, tall, erect, and soldierly, with a direct glance smiles easily and shows his teeth under his brown moustache. About 6ft. in height, near 200 lbs in weight, around 40 years of age."[8] Holmes was married and resided in Victoria, and was an inveterate fisherman. Holmes began by placing a post at Discovery Passage on Vancouver Island's east coast just south of Campbell River and ran his line west to connect with William Ralph's survey of 1892, known as the Ralph Line.

The 1909 Survey to Establish Strathcona Park Boundaries

Twenty-five-year-old James E. Manning, who had logging experience, worked on the 1909 survey as an axeman and wrote an account of the survey work. The survey party that left Victoria, travelling by steamer to Campbell River, numbered twenty-two, and included two "chiefs"—Holmes and Harry Fry. Four Aboriginal men from Duncan were hired as canoemen. Manning remarked that they were good men and friendly. The four Duncan men alternately worked as axemen, and with the other sixteen literally mowed down any trees that stood in the way of running this line; in fact, no tree was allowed to stand on this line no matter how large it was.[9]

Campbell River was a settlement when the surveyors came to do their work, although some parts of the area had previously been divided into lots as the first settler, Fred Nunns, was able to obtain a pre-emption in 1887. This property had initially belonged to Mike and James King, and was free to Nunns in exchange for making a specified number of improvements on it over a specified time period.

The earliest known survey of the area was conducted along the coast and into the Campbell River estuary in 1860 by Captain George Richards and his crew on HMS *Plumper*, an early steam vessel from England. Richards was an experienced hydrographer who was sent to Vancouver Island in 1857 to negotiate with the United States for finalizing the border between the United States and the Colonies of Vancouver Island and British Columbia, and to complete the survey work begun by Captain George Vancouver in 1792. With Vancouver's charts as a guide, Richards and his crew proceeded north from their base in Esquimalt and named several features along the way, for the most part after the ship's officers; however, Richards was mandated to retain Spanish and Indigenous place names where possible. When they reached Quadra Island, they found a protected cove, today's Quathiaski Cove, and from this safe anchorage scouted the Quadra Island and Vancouver Island shorelines. The river they saw on the Vancouver Island side was named the Campbell River after the ship's surgeon, Dr. Samuel Campbell. On their way, they had stopped in the Comox region where they found the K'omoks People of the Comox Valley friendly; they were, however, under the impression that northern tribes, the Laich-Kwil-Tach, whom they referred to as the Euclataw, were to be feared. By this time, the Laich-Kwil-Tach had settled in the Campbell River region and on Quadra Island as the earlier Salish tribes moved south. Perhaps due to the Laich-Kwil-Tach's reputation, settlers weren't inclined to take advantage of the richness of land, where salmon were plentiful and forests thick.[10] In addition, Campbell River had no natural harbour, and in a coastal region where people travelled from place to place by water, settlers found the Discovery Islands more attractive with easier and safer boat access. A government wharf was finally built in Campbell River in 1906, although ships could not tie up there in heavy weather. Just before the survey party visited, Campbell River was joined to Courtenay–Comox by a foot trail, but by 1909, the year the survey party arrived, a rough road had replaced the trail, making it somewhat passable by horse and buggy.[11]

By this time, the Laich-Kwil-Tach or Wei Wai Kum First Nation was restricted to Reserve #11 on the Tyee Spit, a piece of land that jutted out and ran north from the coast, approximately across from Quathiaski Cove, and to Reserve #12 to the west of the main settlement. Nunns' property in Campbellton was adjacent to the Spit, and in his diary he mentions having a dispute with the Laich-Kwil-Tach about the boundary of the property.[12]

Manning met Nunns when the survey party was on the move from their initial beach camp south of Campbell River, where they had stayed for about three weeks, to McIvor Lake, about fifteen

Laich-Kwil-Tach family on the reserve in Campbell River, 1910. IMAGE
MCR006371 COURTESY OF THE MUSEUM AT CAMPBELL RIVER ARCHIVES

kilometres to the west and the end of the road. Manning found
out by conversing with Nunns that a nephew of Nunns was in their
party. The crew initially stayed at the Willows Hotel, considered
to be a fine establishment, before they set up their beach camp.
The hotel and a general store had been built in 1904 by Charles
and Frederick Thulin, brothers from Sweden who established their
first hotel at Lund, on the Malaspina Peninsula on the BC mainland north of Powell River. Their Lund hotel manager, Emerson
Hannan, was a partner in the venture and took over management
of the Willows. The hotel boasted modern amenities such as hot
running water and a sizeable barroom that catered to the loggers
camped nearby, and the lodgings were designed to accommodate
wealthy sports fishermen drawn by the legendary Tyee salmon and
the excellent freshwater fishing in the rivers and lakes.

Manning remarked that the survey crew were happy to get away
from the barroom, either because of the boisterous loggers or perhaps because it was too much of a temptation to spend all their
free time there.

In any event, Hannan from the hotel helped transport the crew's gear with his team of horses and wagon to their new location. The following day, Hannan surprised them with the delivery of a thirty-five-foot canoe purchased from an "Indian Chief." Manning speculated that this canoe "did more to open the back country of this District than any other one thing."[13] Large enough to accommodate sixteen people and their gear, it was in use for several years and was the first such water-going vessel Manning knew of on McIvor Lake.

The survey team backtracked to find the end of the line they had completed in the first part of the survey, and having located it, continued on to place a 12 mile post at Lower Campbell Lake, the next lake west of McIvor. They then moved camp to a spot on the Campbell River between Lower and Upper Campbell Lakes and remarked that a crew had already been cutting rather winding trails toward Buttle Lake, via Gooseneck and the Quinsam Lakes. Manning's group planted the 17 mile post further inland, then had to stop as by this time it was November. Days were getting shorter, colder and wetter.

The survey party returned to Victoria, then the following spring, in 1910, went back to Campbell River under the leadership of Holmes to complete their work. Manning found the settlement of Campbell River to be much the same, but the Willows Hotel was new, replacing the previous one that had burned down toward the end of 1909. This one, he said, "was much more elaborate."[14]

They covered familiar ground to McIvor Lake, glad to find their canoe in good condition, and paddled and hiked west to where they had finished off, only to be met with deep snow and a heavy windfall of trees. This slowed their progress, but they made it to the 20 mile post. Manning remarked that they encountered extremely large red and yellow cedar trees about eight feet across, some of which had to be removed as they were "on the line." They turned south at the 20 mile marker and continued setting up posts at every mile until they reached Allan Creek. Although it was July, due to their elevation they were camping in snow. From there they traversed to the 135 mile post at the Ralph Line to complete the circuit.

When the survey crew returned to McIvor Lake, they were surprised by news from Victoria, brought by a messenger who bore instructions for Holmes. He was to keep as many members of the current party in Campbell River as he could, so that they could join a new party coming from Victoria, whose purpose was to assess whether the reserve set aside by McBride would be suitable as a park.[15]

The Ellison Expedition

This new exploratory party was led by Minister of Lands Price Ellison. Ellison was born in Britain, as were Buttle and Bolton, and lived in the Okanagan, British Columbia's mainland interior, where he farmed his 320-acre property. By 1891, he had secured a reputation for himself as a successful grower of fruits and vegetables and for many years advocated the use of irrigation. Ellison became involved in the community and eventually entered politics. Lindsay Elms, in an article about Ellison, describes him as

> typical of politicians in British Columbia in the late 1800s to early 1900s when they were some of the most corrupt in Canadian history. Ellison went on and used his landholdings as a vehicle toward prosperity. Price Ellison's political success was cultivated by creating an image of integrity, purpose and kindness in the community through the media and public events. He sought political power, social status and influence to ensure that he prospered.[16]

Considering his appetite for owning land, it is interesting that Ellison supported the creation of a wilderness park. Perhaps he saw no agricultural value in the mountainous Strathcona region and, as a witness to how available land throughout the province was disappearing through private ownership, understood the need to set some areas aside as public land. When he came to lead the expedition, "the Chief" Ellison was fifty-eight years old, a large man with a walrus moustache who loved the outdoors and had the leadership qualities and tenacity necessary to make the venture a success.

Ellison, his twenty-year-old daughter Myra, his nephew Harry McClure Johnson who kept a journal of the expedition, photographer Frank Ward who took stunning photographs of the journey, the seasoned explorer Reverend William Bolton, a cook and a packer were among those who came by steamer from Victoria. Reports of the challenges of entering the new reserve from the south via Alberni and Great Central Lake led to the choice of Campbell River as the gateway to the Park. The first leg of their journey was from Victoria to Vancouver on the CPR ship SS *Queen City* on July 5, 1910, where Johnson noted that they picked up numerous supplies and spent some enjoyable time at the Vancouver Hotel, newly built by the CPR, before carrying on to Campbell River.[17] He also observed that while on the water near Savary Island, there was a wonderful view of snow-capped peaks that lay within both the coastal mainland mountain range and the Island's range.

Manning noted that initially there was to be a small select group to make up this new party, but soon a local guide who lived at the Upper Campbell River near the proposed Park, "Lord" Bacon, was added to the numbers, as well as timber cruisers, canoemen and packers. In all, the final party, once they were joined by Holmes and the survey crew who elected to go on this new adventure, numbered twenty-three. Travelling west from the settlement was still considered an enormous undertaking and managed by few, attesting to the hardiness of the survey crew. Fortunately the expedition group could enjoy the Willows Hotel before embarking on their trek into the wilderness.

"It was astonishing," wrote Johnson,

> to find so completely equipped a hostelry so far away from any place of size; brass and iron beds, hot and cold running water in

TOP Ellison Expedition participants on the lower balcony of the Willows Hotel.
IMAGE MCR010089 COURTESY OF THE MUSEUM AT CAMPBELL RIVER ARCHIVES

BOTTOM Totem pole on reserve in Campbell River at the Tyee Spit.
IMAGE MCR009156- COURTESY OF THE MUSEUM AT CAMPBELL RIVER ARCHIVES

many of the rooms, some rooms with bath and en suite, wide verandas overlooking the water; a decidedly up-to-date bar, with tiled floor, handsome mirrors, and ornamental iron ceiling. The Captain [of SS *Queen City*] had told us there was a good hotel, but we had no reason to believe it would be as good as this.

He added that loggers' accommodation was separate from the main hotel so that their rowdy behaviour would not "interfere with patrons of the hotel of quieter instincts." Aside from the hotel, there was "a general store, some scattered buildings and the Indian village on the spit."[18]

From Victoria, the party had brought two canoes, a sixteen footer and twenty-five footer, that with the addition of the thirty-five foot canoe docked at McIvor Lake were to serve the explorers well for the water portion of their travels. Manning noted that cots and special bedding were brought for the "top seven" travellers.[19]

On July 7, the party set out from Campbell River by wagon to McIvor Lake, enduring "six miles of turning and twisting, up and down steep grades." As Johnson noted, it was the only road they would travel on until reaching Alberni. They had consulted with Mike King, who recommended that they make the journey by water rather than rely on any of the new trails being put through. The group took a detour on their way to the lake in order to stop and view the stupendous Campbell River (later Elk) Falls.[20] Johnson raved about the 135-foot-high falls, set in a virgin forest and surrounded by "fragrant firs and lace-leaved cedars," writing:

It not only compares well with those other wonders of a continent and the world in height of tall and volume of water and therefore in majestic grandeur and the wonderful tales it has to tell of the elemental forces of nature, out-rivals the Niagara of today... Anyone standing at the top of the rock wall opposite is drenched by clouds of... spray falling again like heavy rain. Many gorgeous rainbows play in it... The great roar coming down to

The majestic Elk Falls. BETTY BROOKS COLLECTION

you cannot be described. It is like that of the seas, but oh! So much deeper and bigger.[21]

About one mile past the falls they encountered the camp of Horace Smith, a water gauger for the Campbell River Power Company that was started by the King brothers. Smith, whose job it was

Expedition members poling along the Campbell River. IMAGE MCR010104-1

COURTESY OF THE MUSEUM AT CAMPBELL RIVER ARCHIVES

to make an eight-mile trip on the river bank each day to measure the standing water in the river over time, told them, much to the horror of Johnson, that this company had obtained the right to harness the falls to produce hydro-electric power. Johnson felt disbelief that anyone could conceive of exploiting this natural wonder for monetary advantage.

"Soon we may anticipate," he wrote, "these beautiful falls a gift to man from God, to show, shall we say the majesty and sublimity of the Divine Nature, will be transformed into a machine of such-and-such horse power, that will supply light and boards and shingles and shredded wheat to the world."[22] Johnson's words were an eerie foreboding of the eventual battles that would be fought to protect Elk Falls and its forests from development and indeed, subsequently for the protection of the region he was about to explore. Little did he know at the time that despite the success of the expedition he was part of in securing the Strathcona reserve

Lord Bacon's cabin on the lake. IMAGE MCR007122 COURTESY OF THE MUSEUM AT CAMPBELL RIVER ARCHIVES

as park land, only seven years after its creation, amendments would be made to the original Strathcona Park Act to open this ostensibly protected wilderness tract to industrial interests.

The rest of the two-week trip to reach Buttle Lake would be by water, canoeing McIvor, Lower Campbell and Upper Campbell Lakes, at that time all connected by the Campbell River, and fording and portaging the river's many rapids. They were entertained along the way by Lord Bacon, who while full of tall tales, proved to be invaluable due to his intimate knowledge of the river, the lakes and the terrain.[23]

Hugh Nathan Bacon was already a legendary character in the settlement of Campbell River when the expedition hired him as a guide. Thought of as an eccentric fellow who lived alone in the woods west of the settlement in a simple cabin he built himself, with a fox terrier he called "Man," Bacon insisted he was a Lord although he was unable to prove his pedigree. He would inevitably

The "Lord" with his rifle. IMAGE MCR016721 COURTESY OF THE MUSEUM AT CAMPBELL RIVER ARCHIVES

end a story with "and *me* a lord too! What do you think of that? And me a lord!"[24]

A trapper, prospector and guide, he came originally from Scotland, travelled and worked in the United States, then made his way north to the Yukon to chase Klondike gold before coming to Vancouver Island. He apparently once had a wife while in the State of Washington, but she passed away. Stimulated by a drink or two of Scotch, he would entertain patrons of the Willows Hotel bar with recitations from Kipling, while at the same time informing the local loggers that they were a pack of drunkards.

Bill Hall, who went along with Bacon on prospecting trips as a boy of twelve, remembered Bacon well. "He used to say, 'Redress your feet often and make sure you have tea and a can, and you can go a long ways, but without your feet you'll not get far,' and on Bacon's forays into the wilderness he carried nothing but a billy can, tea, hard tack and a hunk of cheese" and of course, spare socks. Sir John Rogers, who met Bacon at the Willows Hotel, said he was "wizened in appearance and lightly built but hard as nails." He was also described as "a... dapper man with light coloured eyes,"[25] and Johnson commented that though Bacon said his age was forty-eight, he appeared older. At five foot five and weighing about 130 pounds, Bacon was a very active man, and despite his apparent age, the younger men of the party sometimes struggled to keep up with him. "He never seems to hurry, yet always gives the impression of speed," Johnson wrote after watching him. "He slides along just like a cat—more properly 'like a cat of the woods,' a cougar, so like a thing of the woods is he, always alert, every muscle under perfect control, always masterful, seeing every exigency before it happens and always ready to meet it."[26]

Any observations made about Bacon and his character are perhaps best exemplified by his role as guide during Ellison's expedition. In this role, both his unsurpassed skill as an outdoorsman and his depth of local knowledge, alongside his myriad of idiosyncrasies, are duly noted by the pen of the keen-eyed Johnson, creating a delightful portrait of one of British Columbia's most endearing originals.

Throughout his journal, Johnson refers to Bacon as either "Lord Hughey" or "Lord B.," noting that Bacon appreciated the young man's attentiveness to his stories. Although Bacon kept up a continuous stream of patter on the journey, his real life and circumstances were somewhat shrouded in mystery, as it was never clear whether or not his many stories were true. Johnson described Bacon's conversation as "a queer combination of sense and nonsense," and remarked that "His constant stream of remarks and anecdotes were as varied as they were unusual."[27] Hall commented that one of his foibles was that he didn't like to sleep outside under a full moon "because he thought it had a bad effect on him."[28] It was generally agreed that Bacon was well-read and conversant on numerous topics, and had in fact written a number of books himself, although the titles of these alleged books changed with each telling. He complained that others tried to bilk him out of his mineral claims, and when they reached his holdings at Iron Mountain, Bacon was circumspect about showing his fellow travellers too much. It seems that at one time he had been shot at over a mineral claim dispute, losing two fingers, but had escaped by jumping into the Quinsam River.[29]

Before they reached Buttle Lake, the party split up so that a select number could attempt the ascent of Crown Mountain, and Bacon stayed behind with the main camp, directed by the "Chief" to have their provisions transferred to near Buttle's Lake in anticipation of the climbers' return. Despite his bad knee, injured in a canoe upset on the river, Ellison was determined to climb the mountain, reminding Johnson that "we have had it in mind to climb Crown Mt. ever since before we left Victoria, if we do little else," and Johnson concurred that their leader's sheer force of will would likely help the venture succeed.[30]

Indeed, the nine intrepid climbers reached the summit on July 29, 1910: Price and Myra Ellison, Colonel Holmes, Charles Haslam, Frank Ward, Lionel Hudson, James Hasworth, Harry McClure

The main camp near the north end of Buttle Lake. IMAGE MCR010119 COURTESY OF THE MUSEUM AT CAMPBELL RIVER ARCHIVES

Johnson and Jim "Scotty" Twaddle. The climbers descended the mountain, and under the guidance of Twaddle, the group made their way towards the main camp.

After exchanging rifle shots with the campers to ascertain their location, they "set out almost hysterically, on a half run even with our packs. Very quickly we are met by Lord Bacon, and behind him Mr. Bolton, who have run breathless from the camp... We have been at such high tension all day that it seems impossible that we are here." A meal was prepared for the climbers, and Johnson commented, "Never had a meal tasted so good."[31]

After a few days' rest, the group set out toward Buttle Lake, visiting Lord Bacon's cabin along the way, which Johnson described as "a poor makeshift" although set in a pretty clearing. By the end of the day, they reached Buttle Lake, which Bolton had already travelled, and were "so lost in our admiration of the lake as we

TOP Sailing on Buttle Lake. IMAGE MCR010134 COURTESY OF THE MUSEUM AT CAMPBELL RIVER ARCHIVES

BOTTOM, LEFT Gravel flats at Myra Falls. WILL J. REID FAMILY COLLECTION

BOTTOM, RIGHT The adult Myra Thompson (née Cliffe) camping near Strathcona Park with baby daughter Myra, circa 1910. MYRNA BOULDING COLLECTION

proceed that we do not notice the flight of time."[32] Two days later, they moved camp to the south end of the lake near Myra Falls, with Johnson remarking, "Is one of the best we have ever had. Underfoot is gravel mostly. About us are fir and balsam and cedars and hemlock, and along the shore alder. The roar of the falls is ever in the background."[33] In a strange twist of fate, they named the river they camped near the Myra River, and the falls Myra Falls, after Ellison's daughter "Miss E.," not knowing Mike King had done the same for Myra Cliffe years earlier.

Two days later, on August 8, they made their way to the place they expected to meet Captain Roberts, who had been blazing a trail for them across "the Great Divide" from Great Central Lake. Bacon's dog Man alerted them to the presence of Roberts, who the party was extremely relieved to intercept. That same day they set out on the new trail with Lord Bacon, who elected to stay with the party. Bolton, the only one who had previously made the traverse, found the next day he wasn't feeling well and asked the "Chief" Ellison if he could return to Buttle Lake. Given permission, he quit the party.

Their ascent up the trail took them into snow and ice, and Johnson estimated that by the end of that day, they had reached an elevation of 4,750 feet. The next day they reached beautiful Margaret Lake, and despite difficulties sleeping there were glad to have seen it. Early on the morning of August 11, they made it to Joe Drinkwater's Ark Hotel at Great Central Lake, and the "Chief" engaged two packers who had been staying there to send telegrams from Alberni to Premier McBride and the party's families to let them know all had arrived safely.

The next day, they reached the community of Alberni, where all were happy to take a bath and find their city clothes waiting for them. Despite looking forward to the comfort of a night in a hotel, Johnson commented that he "had a poor night, because the bedclothes and room seemed to smother me."[34] On the 13th they travelled by automobile to Nanaimo, caught the E & N train and arrived safely back to Victoria to tell their tale.[35]

Joe Drinkwater's Ark Hotel on Great Central Lake. IMAGE PN01064 ALBERNI VALLEY MUSEUM PHOTOGRAPH COLLECTION

The glowing report of the Ellison Expedition participants led McBride in March of 1911 to name the reserve British Columbia's first provincial park.

Strathcona the Beautiful, British Columbia's First Provincial Park

A clear appreciation of Strathcona Park's isolation is important to understanding why the Park had such low visitorship for decades after being established. Once Canada became involved in the First World War, the BC government curtailed all development work, and during the 1920s, the original dream of a tourist mecca at Strathcona gave way to a policy of natural resource exploitation. The goal of improving access to the Park for the benefit of wealthy tourists faded from the provincial government's agenda. Paradoxically, industrial developers and logging companies rather than government built the roads that created better access for all users to the Buttle Lake entrance of the Park.

Even in 1911, the new Park was not free of industrial activity. The explorers in 1910 saw Joe Drinkwater's mine at Big Interior

Mountain, and his was not the only one; there were other Crown-granted mineral claims and active mining development, and Walter Guppy remarks that "the boundaries of this park were established by drawing straight lines on a map apparently with little knowledge of, or concern for what lay within those boundaries."[36]

As well, the Park contained existing timber licences. One of the timber companies that had holdings around Buttle Lake in the newly formed Park was the Victoria Timber and Trading Company Ltd. Fearing public protest, in 1911 the company offered its holdings to the government but was turned down. The province later purchased the licence in April 1939 for $595,000.[37]

Timber companies that had purchased sections of the neighbouring E & N land grant were already cruising the area. Johnson made a reference to a trail blazed from Campbell River by the British America Timber Company and Quinsam Lake Iron Syndicate from Seattle, that would allow the company to reach its timber holdings in the vicinity of Buttle Lake and its mineral claims at Upper Quinsam Lakes.[38] The Cudahy Timber Company and Baxter Pole Company were already logging around Campbell Lake before 1906, when International Timber, whose name changed in 1929 to Elk River Timber, moved inland from the coast and purchased E & N land. By the 1930s, the company would become a presence in the Elk River Valley and at Upper Campbell and Buttle Lakes, logging the northwest corner of Buttle Lake that was outside Park boundaries.

Although the Strathcona Park Act prohibited prospecting and claim staking, a clause stated that persons with any vested rights would not be deprived of them after the Park's formation, and work continued at Joe Drinkwater's Ptarmigan mine site. In 1918, after lobbying from miners, the restrictions on prospecting minerals were lifted.[39] Pro-mining rhetoric of the time included such comments as "most of us are inclined to look at the digging out of our minerals and their utilization from a patriotic viewpoint."[40] While this amendment seemed to favour mining, numerous other amendments to the Act over the years would create confusion about the right to actually work mineral claims.

The industry topmost in the minds of the Park's creators was tourism. The McBride administration hired Seattle engineer Reginald H. Thomson to develop the Park as a tourist mecca, due to his experience in large projects in the United States. Thomson's reputation as an honest, persistent and extremely hard worker was garnered during his years as city engineer for Seattle, Washington. He tackled complicated projects that involved building sewers, levelling the city's hills, securing its water supply and lighting its streets, and he worked outside the city engineering canal construction.[41]

His first task as Strathcona Park engineer was to "secure access to, and into, the rugged, isolated park."[42] At that time, the points of access to the Park, all difficult, were from Alberni to the southwest, the Bedwell Valley to the west, Gold River and Campbell River. Thomson at first envisioned access from Alberni, which had the advantage of road access to Victoria, but once he undertook the trip himself, he recognized the difficulty of crossing the divide travelled by the Ellison party and abandoned the idea.[43] The provincial government therefore undertook building a road west from Campbell River to the Buttle Lake region in 1912. The surveyor Holmes in 1913 described the route:

> A wagon road, at present a very poor one, runs from Campbell River in a westerly direction about 7 miles to McIvor Lake, and thence around this lake for another two miles to Forbes Landing at the east end of Lower Campbell Lake; thence it continues as a horse-trial via Gooseneck Lake along Upper Campbell Lake and Upper Campbell River to Buttle Lake, within park limits. Along this trail a first-class road is at present under construction, which it is expected will be completed in about two years, giving easy access to Buttle Lake for those on pleasure bent.[44]

"All Roads Lead to Strathcona Park"

R.H. Thomson's 1914 progress report concerning planning for the Park contains details of the road construction, and his enthusiasm

The road heading west from the settlement of Campbell River toward Strathcona Park, circa 1920. IMAGE MCR006950 COURTESY OF THE MUSEUM AT CAMPBELL RIVER ARCHIVES

for the undertaking is plain to see when he remarks that as all roads lead to Rome, "all roads lead to Strathcona Park."[45] Eric Sismey, an early surveyor on the road referred to by Holmes, described his journey to the surveyor's camp at Gooseneck Lake, marvelling at the enormous trees he passed on the way. Sismey stayed at the

Gooseneck Lake surveyor's camp for roughly a year. While Holmes was "blazing the park boundaries," Sismey's group surveyed the proposed route along Lower Campbell and Upper Campbell Lakes to Buttle Lake, and developed pack horse trails along the Campbell River. Once the existing horse trail became a serviceable road, his crew forged a trail into the Park that extended past the end of the surveyed road, until November rains prohibited further work.[46]

By 1915, the road itself was completed to within about eleven miles of the Park's entrance. Two years later, Wallace Baikie travelled the road that he described as having sections as wide as thirty-three feet, although Thomson reported that the majority of the road was 14.6 feet wide. At twenty miles long, the road terminated near Jasper Sutherland's provisioning camp on the shores of Upper Campbell Lake, from where it was possible to get a boat and travel by water to the end of Upper Campbell Lake, then complete the trip to the Park by hiking in nine miles to Buttle Lake. Jasper and his two brothers, Walter and Bill, came to the Campbell River region in 1912 and that year assisted Jim Forbes, who had built a campsite on Lower Campbell Lake, with building his first lodge, Forbes Landing. Then they built their own provisioning camp on Upper Campbell Lake. Together with Forbes, from 1913 to 1915, they ferried supplies to Holmes' surveyors, who stayed in a cabin at the outlet of Buttle Lake and worked on building trails in and around Strathcona Park. After the surveyors left, the provisioners made use of the survey trails and would act as guides to those who wanted to visit the Park.[47]

Baikie also commented that the government had an ambitious scheme for "beautifying" the wilderness route that included planting roughly 3,000 trees and 10,000 plants (including the invasive Scotch broom), and sowing 400 pounds of seeds, at the same time as magnificent old growth trees were being cut and burned at the side of the road as work proceeded. Baikie was astonished at the waste and estimated that government road engineers could have earned the government $12,000 in revenue from the "fine timber" they were burning.[48]

Jasper, Walter and Bill Sutherland's provisioning camp on Upper Campbell Lake. MYRNA BOULDING COLLECTION

Sismey wrote that the surveyors entertained numerous well-known people who were attracted to the region, as Strathcona Park had been "advertised far and wide" even though the Park was officially closed.[49] Some of these visitors had in fact been specifically invited by the engineer Thomson. He organized selective promotion by such groups as the Alpine Club of Canada, who in return wrote glowing reports of their journey in the *Canadian Alpine Journal*.[50] The lucky few who managed to get to the Park would report how Buttle Lake "just boiled with fish." The Ellison party in 1910 recorded having caught an astonishing seventy trout in Buttle Lake in one evening's fishing during their expedition.[51]

Despite the growing interest in visiting the Park among those with the income and leisure to undertake the journey, construction on the highway ceased in 1915, a year after the First World War broke out. Funds were diverted away from the project toward the war effort, and a lack of manpower, as road crews enlisted or were conscripted, further inhibited progress. It is interesting to speculate whether finances from timber sales would have encouraged officials to push the road to completion. Historian William Wilson notes that resentment of Thomson's non-Canadian status as well as his high salary contributed to his decision to return to the US in 1915.[52]

The dream of using the Park to promote tourism on Vancouver Island did not die altogether despite the war. A deputation of Island civic elites met with Premier Richard McBride and Minister of Public Works Thomas Taylor on November 1915 in Victoria. Some expressed hopes that with tourists cut off from Europe because of the current conflict, the North American continent would become an inviting tourist destination, offering soothing wilderness respite from the vagaries of war. Herbert Cuthbert of the Tourist Association of Victoria submitted figures to show that tourism had become an industry, and the expansion of rail construction in the Pacific Northwest of the United States was bound to benefit Vancouver Island.[53] He believed it was critical for the Island to expand its own rail transportation system beyond Nanaimo, as well as to have road work completed in the north central part of the Island. McBride and Taylor made it clear, however, that there would be no further development of Strathcona Park "as would put that area in such shape as to make it available for tourists and warrant advertising it as a tourist resort. The need of conserving the financial resources of the Province to meet urgent expenditures in other directions precluded any considerable outlay on Strathcona Park."[54] McBride told the deputation it would cost at least another $300,000 to complete the work. His compromise was to promise that the Provincial Bureau of Information would issue an illustrated Strathcona Park promotional pamphlet. Another attendee claimed, in error, that there was a good motor road "to within three miles of the park."[55] This misinformation about the distance to be completed no doubt caused the deputation to wonder why the work could not be done,

A car broken down on the rough road near Sutherland's camp. IMAGE
MCR008065 COURTESY OF THE MUSEUM AT CAMPBELL RIVER ARCHIVES

with others suggesting the use of interned German aliens and returning soldiers to perform the labour.[56]

As promised, in 1916 a promotional pamphlet entitled *Strathcona the Beautiful* was produced by the Bureau of Information. However, it misled readers about the ease of getting to the Park, claiming that a motorist could drive an automobile all the way from Victoria to Campbell River, when in fact Courtenay was the northern terminus of the Island Highway.[57] With the war over in 1919, groups such as the Island Automobile Association were lobbying for the opening up of roads to such destinations as Strathcona Park.[58]

In that same year, Campbell River was at last connected to Victoria by road via Courtenay. There was now an alternative to having to take a coastal steamer to get to Campbell River, but the journey to the Park was a distance of about thirty miles, and since stoppage of work on the road to the Park in 1915, access from Campbell River itself had not been improved upon.

While the provincial government may have had no intention of completing the road to the Park and connecting it to the trails constructed by Holmes' crew at Buttle Lake, local interests in the 1920s continued to lobby for improvements. A writer reporting from Campbell River lamented in the *Daily Colonist* in 1922 that "only eleven miles of road require to be constructed to allow automobiles to reach the lower end of Buttle's Lake most of which is included in Strathcona Park."[59] The state of the road west of Campbell River was thus described in a *Comox Argus* article of 1923: "The road from Courtenay to Forbes Landing and seven miles beyond it is in good condition... But the last seven miles at the end of the road is bad, and anyone going over it is doing so at the risk of broken springs."[60] The road completed by the government in 1915 had clearly deteriorated in the intervening years, since the entire route from Forbes Landing to where the road ended at Upper Campbell Lake was driveable at that time. Indeed, a 1915 government report predicted that if work on the road was delayed, it would inevitably become obliterated once subjected to the region's heavy rains.[61]

The Courtenay Board of Trade and Associated Boards of Trade of Vancouver Island, citing the increasing volume of tourist traffic in the region, continued to urge the opening up of the Park. Their 1924 Resolution observed that "to carry the road through to Strathcona Park would cost a considerable amount of money; but to finish it to Upper Campbell Lake is comparatively inexpensive and should be done at once." Again in 1925, the local Board of Trade argued that since so much money had already been spent on constructing the Strathcona Park road, and since such a road would be an asset to the province, it should be completed regardless of cost. Minister of Lands T.D. (Duff) Pattullo responded that the province had no immediate interest in constructing a road to Strathcona Park.[62] A year later, the *Colonist* wondered if the government would develop Strathcona or cancel its designation as a park.[63]

Certainly the Department of Lands had no budget and no intention of building roads to parks or building trails within parks.[64] Yet even so, the province's first tourist brochures, Park Guide Books, were printed in 1921 by the Ministry of Lands. For Strathcona, this would be a new and revised pamphlet that described the wonders of Strathcona Park with precise travel instructions, making it clear that "There is no road at present into the Park." No automobiles could go past Sutherland's Camp, and from that point on there was only a pack trail to Buttle Lake.[65] The difference was that in 1921, five years after the printing of the 1916 pamphlet, it *was* possible to drive to Campbell River.

Like the first promotional pamphlet, the 1921 version emphasized the Park's natural beauty in glowing terms, and described in detail how to reach Buttle Lake:

The Esquimalt & Nanaimo Railway extends from Victoria to Courtenay, 146 miles, about 30 miles south of Campbell River. Coasting steamers from Victoria and Vancouver make regular calls at Campbell River, a village with good hotel accommodation, stores, etc., business centre and port of a farming, logging, and fishing community of about 500 people, and famous among anglers. Forbes Landing, where a good hotel, and large garage where motors can be stored, skirts the shore of Lower Campbell Lake, is 9 miles from Campbell River, and a short branch from the Campbell River-Forbes Landing Road leads to Elk Falls, where a mighty volume plunges over a series of falls, the highest 120 feet, into a seething cauldron of rainbow-tinted mist and spray with a roar audible a mile distant. At Campbell River and Forbes Landing guides can be engaged, and a pack-train operates

ABOVE, LEFT Beautiful Buttle Lake, looking south from a gravel beach on the west side. WILL J. REID FAMILY COLLECTION

ABOVE, RIGHT Young adults Rose Baikie, Myra Thompson and Wallace Baikie hiking in Strathcona Park in 1925. MYRNA BOULDING COLLECTION

from Forbes Landing each summer, information regarding its movements and costs, etc., being obtainable at Forbes Hotel.

Motors can travel to within a mile of Upper Campbell Lake, or about 12 miles beyond Forbes Landing, but there is no accommodation to store cars beyond that place. From the end of the road a trail follows along the southerly side of Campbell Lake and the east side of Campbell River to Buttle Lake. This trail is suitable for horses. There are some log cabins provided where travellers going in on foot or horseback may shelter, also camping-sites beside the trout-filled streams and lake. At Buttle Lake is a sleeping-cabin with accommodation for twenty-six, equipped with a stove, and a special room for ladies. Distance by road and trail from Campbell River to Buttle Lake is 34 miles, over half by road. An alternate trail leaving the road at Gooseneck Lake runs via Upper Quinsam Lake. Branch trails lead from the main trail up Elk River and its forks via the valleys between the mountains, and trails from Buttle Lake lead to points of interest in the surrounding alpine area. Some rowboats are kept on Buttle Lake.

A decade after the pamphlet was published, another *Colonist* writer linked Strathcona's isolation to the broader frustration at the slow pace of road construction all over the Island, particularly the north end. "A quarter of a century ago Strathcona Park was set aside to become the great playground of North America. Not a pick has been turned in that area in twenty-two years."[66] After he made a visit eight years later, the *Colonist's* Frank Kelley believed that Strathcona would "appeal to a large number seeking healing for sick minds and jaded nerves." Like so many others, he wondered why "something has not been done to open this park area for the benefit of present-day folk," since only a short section of road was required to access the Buttle Lake entrance to the Park.[67]

It is perhaps due to the potential for hydro-electric development in Strathcona Park that the provincial government from the 1920s onward hesitated to develop either the Park or the road for the benefit of recreationists. In fact, this attitude applied to all provincial parks. An amendment to the Parks Act in 1924 allowed for the acquisition of lands and permission to exchange timber for land and applied to parks with no governing board.[68] Also in 1924, the Water Rights Branch of the provincial Department of Lands sent its hydrological engineer Frederick Knewstubb to do the field work and report on the hydro-electric potential of the Campbell River watershed. He visited Elk Falls and determined that should the power of the falls be harnessed, there should be three reservoirs created to sustain the necessary flow: one at Lower Campbell Lake, the second at Upper Campbell Lake and the third at Buttle Lake. Despite this recommendation, in his description of Buttle Lake he made it clear that his personal opinion was that this exquisite setting should not be altered by raising water levels.

> Buttle Lake has a natural setting of exceptional beauty. The fishing appears to be excellent, and there are numerous flats with gravel beaches along its shores which would make excellent camping sites. It was intended by the then Government to develop the natural features as far as possible, and it was probably considered that any use of the lake which would involve raising its surface could not but be detrimental to its use for park

Elk River Timber Camp 9 on the west shore of Upper Campbell Lake. IMAGE
MCR013061 COURTESY OF THE MUSEUM AT CAMPBELL RIVER ARCHIVES

purposes. In this view most person after seeing this lake, would
concur. Any step which would mar the natural beauty of the lake
or flood the low-lying flats and beaches, especially if such flooding extended over the holiday season, would not escape a good
share of execration.[69]

Despite Knewstubb's reservations about desecrating the beauty
of Buttle Lake, in 1927 the statute was changed so that water levels
within Strathcona Park would be allowed to rise, coinciding with
American pulp and paper company Crown Willamette's interest
in harnessing the power of Elk Falls and creating the reservoirs, as
recommended by Knewstubb, in order to power a proposed Campbell River mill. The last reservoir would be Buttle Lake. As park
historian James Anderson wrote, the changes to the Act "made
the creation, reduction and abolition, the flooding, the mining and
logging of parks a simple matter of the stroke of a pen." Any park
infrastructure such as campsites, cabins or trails would be lost in
flooding or would have to be moved.[70]

The lack of a proper road west would not keep locals from driving to the excellent fishing and hunting grounds in the Strathcona vicinity, and logging companies played a role in opening up access to the interior of the Island to the public. With tidewater timber becoming less abundant in the 1920s, logging companies sought tracts farther inland. Railway logging began in earnest in the 1920s, and rail lines extended over much of north central Vancouver Island. From Menzies Bay, just north of Campbell River, and from Campbellton on the northwest side of Campbell River, lines ran to International Timber's (Elk River Timber after 1929) Camp 8 at Echo Lake, situated between Forbes Landing resort and Gooseneck Lake.

"It was a railroad show," wrote Helen Mitchell, "and the company built many miles of roads in the hills around the Campbell and Quinsam Lakes and, as time passed, beyond that deep into the Elk River Valley."[71] Beyond Camp 8, rail lines ran along the east shore of Upper Campbell Lake and across a trestle to the west shore to Camp 9, also an Elk River Timber camp. In the 1940s, Elk River Timber constructed rail lines crossing the Elk River delta south into Buttle Lake. In an effort to make use of the steel it already owned (it would take up unused steel and situate it where they wanted new lines), Elk River Timber planned in the early 1950s to extend the rail from Camp 9 going west, following the Elk River to their holdings in Gold River. For the time being, it was utilizing a rough logging road built above the west side of Upper Campbell Lake that reached its holdings on the west coast.[72]

Where logging roads had been built along the Campbell Lakes, they were private; however, hunters, anglers and hikers made use of them, and these roadways would take them further west than the original 1915 government road would.[73]

Even as the logging industry improved automobile access west of Campbell River, it remained difficult to reach Buttle Lake. The original pack trail constructed by Colonel Holmes and his crew, that reached from Upper Campbell Lake to Buttle Lake,[74] and the 1930s trail were partially obliterated by Elk River Timber's logging activity. The assistant forester for the Parks Division, Dominic Mickle (Mickey) Trew, outlined in his 1950 reconnaissance report that the timber companies themselves recognized the challenge with timber licences around Buttle Lake.[75]

> In 1936 the company owning the remainder of the timber at the north end of Buttle Lake, outside the park, tried to induce the Government to acquire it to preserve access to the lake. This offer was not accepted then, but public pressure in 1940 forced the acquisition by exchange of the remaining unlogged blocks. The exchange covered Blocks 122–125 and involved approximately $35,000 worth of timber. Although preserved from logging, the area has not been integrated into Strathcona Park and might simply be considered as "reserved for recreational purposes."... not all land but the rest belongs to E & N still.
>
> ... in the rest of the park, three areas covered by alienated leases have been logged without much attention by the public. These areas are the holdings of: Bloedel, Stewart and Welch Logging Company of Drinkwater Creek; those of Alberni Pacific Logging Company in the headwaters of Ash River; and those of the Elk River Timber Company on the Elk River.[76]

Local conservationist and renowned author Roderick Haig-Brown explained in a *Victoria Times* article that "the excellent pack trail on which the public works department had spent thousands of dollars in the 1930s was logged over and closed."[77] Frustrated by the lack of jurisdictional cooperation, he went on to say that "no government department would admit responsibility—the forestry did not need it for protection, the public works had right of way, the parks division could spend no money outside the park area."[78]

Haig-Brown came to Campbell River in the late 1930s and settled with his Seattle-born wife, Ann, "in the place farthest north that he could where his city wife could still have a bath."[79] Over the next forty years, he lived next to, listened to and fished the Campbell River. In this place, he rose to prominence as a writer on

The landscape after logging at the edge of Buttle Lake in the late 1930s. WILL J. REID FAMILY COLLECTION

angling, frequently penning acerbic observations on how industry practices and short-sighted government policies threatened the fish and wildlife of Vancouver Island.[80] Strathcona Park became a special place to him and he was vocal about its unique attractions, in particular Buttle Lake and the fine fishing, beautiful trees and beaches for picnicking.

Strathcona Park in 1939 was administered differently from most provincial parks that had been taken over by the Parks Division of the BC Forest Service. The three statute parks of the province, Strathcona, Mount Robson and Garibaldi, would remain under the authority of the Department of Lands. Also in 1939, under the Forest Act, a new classification scheme for parks was created: Class A parks were protected from exploitation; in Class B parks, prospecting, mining and logging were allowed; and Class C was a designation created for picnic and playground parks. No mining would be allowed in Class A parks, but the rules governing logging were somewhat ambiguous, stating that cutting timber "may be necessary or advantageous in developing or improving the parks or protecting and preserving the major values of the parks for enjoyment."[81] The timber could not be sold for revenue. This same Forest Act was amended to give cabinet authority to "constitute... extend, reduce or cancel" any provincial park, which would eventually have consequences for both Elk Falls Provincial Park and Strathcona.[82]

The Parks Division in fact had no interest in developing Strathcona Park in the 1940s. Chester (Chess) Lyons, the Division's first employee, was hired in 1942 as an engineer and explained that the Division's interest was in developing small parks on Vancouver Island that would be easily accessible to the public. Strathcona Park, he said, "Was back there and out of sight, out of mind. It might as well have been in Alaska."[83]

While various departments within government had no interest in improving access to or infrastructure within the Buttle Lake region in the 1940s, there was activity at the lake of a different nature.

LOGGERS, TRESPASSERS AND MILLIONAIRES

From the camp-site on Buttle Lake another journey can be made by taking a launch up the lake, listening to the roar of the cascades and seeing the feathery veil of water falling over the precipices, to the foot of Myra Falls, with fish-pools at the foot and on the terraces. The trail climbs up to the terraces, where cascade after cascade foams down the steps, and thence runs through a narrow, timbered, charming valley with a wondrous array of flora to a flowery meadow beside a lake at the head, where the traveler camps. The shores of Wolf Lake are so steep near the outlet that it is necessary to climb to some height to get easy going. The outlet is over picturesque waterfalls and cascades.

STRATHCONA PARK, VANCOUVER ISLAND
pamphlet from the BC Department of Lands, 1921

THE NEGLECTED PARK was enjoyed by a few squatters and owners of mineral claims who erected cabins or simple camps on the shores of Buttle Lake, and by other individuals who would purchase property for seasonal homes and businesses adjacent to the Park in the Elk River Valley and along Upper Campbell Lake.

The Sutherland brothers maintained their provisioning camp on Upper Campbell Lake into the 1940s, but Lord Bacon's cabin was possibly long gone as no visitors to the area in the '30s or '40s mention seeing it. Charlie Renecker, who Wallace Baikie became friends with while they were both logging, lived on the opposite side of the lake to the Sutherlands. With his partner Alex Brackett, Renecker had purchased 1,100 acres (Lot 259) in the swampy area composed mostly of cedar at the mouth of the Elk River that bordered on the Elk River Timber road near Camp 9. Baikie described him as a "fine specimen [of] manhood, six feet tall, 200 pounds and well muscled" and in personality a "Bull of the Woods."[1] He also commented that Renecker was very active with the Masons, holding a high office.

Renecker and Brackett had purchased the property so they could access barberry bark, from which they made a cascara tincture that was good for many ailments, and this, along with salvaging used railway spikes, became Renecker's main source of income. A rustic cabin was erected close to shore, accessed by a long boardwalk Renecker had built from the cabin over the swamp to the open water where he kept his boat.[2] Baikie's daughters Myrna Boulding and Joanne Campbell remembered visiting Renecker when they were children, as they were both apprehensive about falling off the long boardwalk, only one plank wide, which seemed to go on forever.[3]

Also on that side of the lake, a beautiful cedar lodge was built in 1930 for a millionaire tailor from San Francisco and his wife for $7,000. This was to be their summer wilderness retreat. Myrna Boulding described the couple as "of Swedish stock, blond and vitally handsome." She visited the 54-by-32-foot lodge with her father Wallace during one of his fishing trips to Upper Campbell Lake and remembered how enchanted she was when she saw the stunning interior of the building, with its "four-square pitched ceiling, dramatized and strengthened by open beams, criss-crossed like the lines of the Union Jack, to throw fascinating fire-light shadows." The architect of this masterpiece, she wrote, was Norwegian Jack Earsland. Local carpenters who built the lodge included the Sutherland brothers and Jack Phillips. Mr. Henning Berg died suddenly, and his widow sold the lodge to Mr. and Mrs. Whittaker of Victoria, who named the building Strathcona Lodge and operated it as an exclusive resort.[4]

Wallace Baikie and all the extended family, still residing in Comox, came to vacation in the area for several years, staying at Sutherland's cabins. Then in the early 1940s the Baikie Brothers Logging Company, composed of Wallace and his brothers Harper and Jack, purchased Lot 846, and in the late '40s, with the help of Charlie Renecker, had a large cabin built at Dolly Varden Point that became a favourite family gathering place. The cabin would later also double as a cookhouse while the brothers logged their purchase. Hearing rumours that the John Hart hydro-electric project might extend into Upper Campbell Lake, and all the buildings would be lost to flooding, the Baikies designed their cabin and logging operation bunkhouses so that they could easily float.

On Buttle Lake, within Park boundaries, there were a few cabins, some seasonal and some year-round, built for the most part on

TOP Strathcona Lodge on the west side of Upper Campbell Lake, 1930s.
MYRNA BOULDING COLLECTION

BOTTOM Interior of Strathcona Lodge. MYRNA BOULDING COLLECTION

Con Reid, at left, with Will Reid. WILL J. REID FAMILY COLLECTION

mineral claims. Although today, erecting a building on a claim is prohibited, at that time there were no clear rules in the Mineral Act that prohibited this construction. According to the Parks Department, however, anyone who erected a cabin or summer home was considered to be a trespasser, whether they legally owned a claim or not. In all, there were twenty-seven mineral claims held in the Buttle Lake area. Sixteen were Crown granted, six were staked claims in good standing and five were leased. The leased claims were allowed under the Mineral Act, with the confusing proviso that they came with no surface rights.[5]

John Sutton, who owned a funeral home in Comox, kept a cabin near Myra Falls. Described as "a stoutish man of urbane temper and kindly disposition," Sutton generally came to Buttle Lake in the fall when hunting deer and fishing were good.[6]

Harry Rogers had a cabin on the west side of Buttle Lake near Block 123 on E & N land outside the Park. A journalist, Jack Hames, who met him in the '30s described him as "a typical sourdough in the real sense," who offered his visitors sourdough bread sandwiches for lunch and sourdough pancakes for breakfast. Even his hounds ate sourdough and enjoyed trout from the lake. Rogers was a cougar hunter and trapper, and was described as an immaculate housekeeper.[7]

A gentleman by the name of Con Reid, a friend of Rogers, had built a cabin at Buttle Lake where he lived alone with his dog Barney, which accompanied him on cougar hunts. A 1938 newspaper article described Reid as a "blue-eyed salt," a refugee from Russian-ruled Finland who escaped his country on board a Baltic trawler. According to the journalist, Reid saw the world working and travelling on various seagoing vessels in an era when they were still predominately powered by sail. He received his Scottish name, Reid, when the ship he was on was about to enter Finnish waters and he changed his name to avoid getting caught. He eventually made his way to Canada and served in the Canadian forces during the First World War. Reid ended up on Vancouver Island, where he had a home in Campbell River by the sea and his cabin at the lake, and made a living as a trapper and boat builder.[8]

In 1929, an American lawyer, Louis Titus, and his wife, Alice, purchased a mineral claim at Titus Mountain on the west shore of Buttle Lake, near the mouth of the Wolf River. The Tituses could afford to construct several attractive buildings at this site that were described in a newspaper article that, although not dated, would have been written before 1932, as that year the Titus family had Jim Forbes temporarily oversee the property and open it to tourists.[9]

"We walked up the beach," the writer recounted,

to the owner's dwelling, counting the dozen or so buildings in this pretty group, appraising the excellent workmanship of the rough and hewn logs, gratified with the general air of shipshape homeliness and comfort that pervaded the whole place. Half a mile back in the forest is a lake and brook dammed to give a head for the simple waterworks system which supplies houses and garden. City plumbing and hot water heating installed throughout

ABOVE The Titus Family's Camp Alicia in 1934. WILL J. REID FAMILY COLLECTION

OPPOSITE, TOP William Reid's Seabee amphibious plane. WILL J. REID FAMILY COLLECTION

OPPOSITE, BOTTOM Elk River Timber train tracks at Buttle Narrows. WILL J. REID FAMILY COLLECTION

all brought in by packhorse via the Campbell River, Campbell Lake route.

Split cedar boards, stained and varnished to a beautiful finish, provide most of the interior panels; boulders from the lakeside furnished the stone for a magnificent fireplace in a grand livingroom that commands a view, north and south of fifteen miles of the lake.[10]

Known as Camp Alicia, named for Titus's wife, Alice, the summer residence's guestbook shows an impressive number of visitors from such far-ranging places as San Francisco, Los Angeles and Vancouver as well as nearby Campbell River.[11]

This mineral claim on Blocks 448 and 449 in the Nootka District was sold in 1935 to William J. Reid, the president of Hancock Oil in California, who met Titus at Washington, DC, when they were both working there as consultants. Reid came to Buttle Lake

TOP A young James Hancock at Nootka Lodge. WILL J. REID FAMILY COLLECTION

BOTTOM, LEFT Unidentified young woman with her catch. WILL J. REID FAMILY COLLECTION

BOTTOM, RIGHT Will Reid fly fishing. WILL J. REID FAMILY COLLECTION

for visits and was enthralled by it. With his Seabee float plane, he had the ability to access the lake and did not have to rely on rough roads or neglected trails to get there. Later Reid would purchase Block 419 at the south end of the lake, which he called Loon Point.

Reid improved upon the property with additional buildings and had frequent visits from friends and family, whose way he paid. His nephew James Hancock, son of his wife Ella's brother, travelled from Long Beach, California, to Buttle Lake for the first time in 1946, when he was just fourteen years old. The journey was a "huge adventure," he said, beyond anything he'd experienced.[12]

He remembered flying into the Comox airport, that he realized was not like any commercial airport he'd ever seen. Established just four years earlier, it was part of the Comox Air Base. From here, his uncle Will Reid picked him up in his Seabee, a twin-engine amphibious plane that belonged to Reid's company, Hancock Oil. When they arrived at Buttle Lake, they docked at the property the family called Nootka Lodge. Hancock made a total of four visits to Buttle Lake, and his sister also undertook a trip, coming into the lake on a logging train. From the young Hancock's point of view, aside from his uncle's cabins, there was nothing at Buttle Lake. The region was "total wilderness" without a "sign of anything or anybody," and the area had not experienced a "touch of a human hand."[13]

He recalled a large open building constructed to store boats in the off season, and aside from the main cabin there was a cabin for the cook and housekeeper Frances Fisher, and a sauna the family referred to as a Finnish bath. Another small cabin was called "Con's cabin," where Con Reid (no relation) stayed when he was caretaking the property. James Hancock visited Harry Rogers, another caretaker, who was referred to as the "squatter," likely as he was staying on E & N land without permission, and Hancock was treated to his famous sourdough pancakes.

Fishing was popular with everyone who stayed at Nootka Lodge, and the boats were always ready to go out for fishing excursions. Hancock caught a twenty-four-inch trout at Myra Falls where they went for his birthday, but otherwise recalled that the trout were small, not usually more than twelve inches long. His uncle Will Reid theorized that there were too many fish in the lake and not enough food for them, and this resulted in them not growing to capacity.

Hancock believes that Reid was a conservationist two generations ahead of his time.[14] Reid was concerned about deforestation and was an advocate for the protection of wildlife and active with Ducks Unlimited. Educated in Canada at the University of Alberta, he became involved in protecting wetlands in Alberta and the other prairie provinces, buying huge tracts of land for waterfowl habitat. Money raised by Ducks Unlimited in the US went into the Canadian venture. He had seen the destruction of bird habitat in his native United States, and saw an opportunity to prevent that from happening in Canada.

Will Reid was an avid fisherman, and Hancock said he enjoyed getting away in his boat with his fly rod and his dog. Reid had a small skiff to run about the lake in and could explore its many tributaries and scenic areas. His daughter, Virginia, took numerous photos of their excursions. At his cabin site he built a cooler that circulated cool air where fresh fish would be hung, and a smoker so that he could preserve his catch.

During his eighteen years of coming to Buttle Lake, Reid worked behind the scenes protecting park values. He read the books of Roderick Haig-Brown, which James Hancock has seen in the library kept at Nootka Lodge. In 1939, Reid began a correspondence with the local author, and in what was likely the first letter to Haig-Brown, Reid mentioned his admiration for Haig-Brown's writing. However, he wanted to discuss a rumour he had heard about logging operations being planned nearby. In the following letter, neatly typed on Hancock Oil letterhead, Reid appeals to Haig-Brown for assistance:

TOP, LEFT Ella Reid (Will's wife) on horseback with fish basket in front of saddle. WILL J. REID FAMILY COLLECTION

TOP, RIGHT Charles Reid Gaylord with his hand on a grazing deer. WILL J. REID FAMILY COLLECTION

MIDDLE, LEFT Dog "Barney" with skinned bear by a cabin door. WILL J. REID FAMILY COLLECTION

MIDDLE, RIGHT Picnickers on the flats near Myra Falls. WILL J. REID FAMILY COLLECTION

BOTTOM, LEFT Swimmers in Buttle Lake at the base of Myra Falls. WILL J. REID FAMILY COLLECTION

BOTTOM, RIGHT Canadian Pacific floatplane at the dock, for chartered trip to lake. WILL J. REID FAMILY COLLECTION

July 20, 1939

Dear Mr. Haig-Brown:

It made me very sad this summer to learn that logging operations on Upper Campbell River and Lower Buttle were contemplated.

I talked with a Mr. A. G. McLean of Campbell River about the approaching devastation and he suggested that I write to you.

While I have only had the pleasure of a casual acquaintance with you personally, I feel that I do know you well—not only through mutual friends but because of the many enjoyable hours your books have given me.

One of my friends, resident of San Francisco, widely travelled, familiar with Switzerland, Norway, Sweden and other beauty spots of our own Continent, told me not long ago that Buttle Lake was the most beautiful lake he has ever visited. He was at Buttle in 1930.

The Provincial Government acted wisely in setting aside the Plateau and Lake as a sanctuary and a Park. I am hoping that the men who had vision enough to create Strathcona Park can be interested in helping preserve the beauty of the only natural entrance to the Park.

If all other means of preventing the logging operations fail, do you think it might be possible to persuade the logging company to save the trees on each side of the River and on the shore of the Lake for say five hundred feet back from the water?

Forest fires, terrible as they are, do not despoil nature as much as the logging operations commonly used on Vancouver Island and I am hoping against hope that some way may be found to preserve the natural beauty of the country above Upper Campbell Lake.

With Kindest Regards,

I am, Will J. Reid[15]

Nootka Lodge. WILL J. REID FAMILY COLLECTION

View of Reid property looking south. WILL J. REID FAMILY COLLECTION

Haig-Brown responded on July 31 of that same year that he had spoken with an engineer from Elk River Timber, a friend of his who said he hadn't heard anything about operations planned at Buttle Lake. However, a letter of the following spring dated March 30 reveals Haig-Brown heard that the British American Timber Company that had originally purchased the E & N land grant property in the area with the intention to log had recently sold its holdings, but that the work would be concentrated farther south outside the Park at Oyster Bay. He optimistically felt there was time before this operation reached the Park. He also informed Reid he believed "the Provincial Government bought all the timber licences held along Buttle Lake within the Park boundaries in 1929. There should be some chance," he continued, "of arguing that no timber anywhere along the lake or along the approach to the lake should be touched; this second point is in line with a government policy already declared of 'protecting stands of timber along new roads wherever possible.'"[16]

Haig-Brown also responded in this same letter to Reid's invitation to visit Nootka Lodge. He didn't think a visit was possible, citing that he and his wife could not get away as they often had a large number of visitors in the summer.

Although Reid's early concerns of 1939 might have seemed premature, in 1942 he found out that Elk River Timber intended to log its holdings at the north end of Buttle Lake, a section from the old E & N land grant not yet incorporated into the Park. He asked for assistance from a friend and former American politician, Harvey E. Harris, to engage in a dialogue with the Minister of Lands and Forests, Arthur Wellesley (Wells) Gray about this potential blight on the viewscape. Harris invited Gray to visit the site of the proposed logging and was able to mitigate the problem by negotiating an agreement for a 400-foot fringe of trees to be left around the logged over area at the shores of Buttle Lake.[17] It was at that time, however, that the trail used to access the Park was destroyed.

There was worse to come. Changes were made in Elk Falls Provincial Park, authorized by the Lieutenant-Governor-in-Council under the Electric Power Act, to divert Elk Falls around this time. A newly created government body, the BC Power Commission, was mandated to amalgamate existing power corporations and "to extend service to all parts of the province."[18]

"THE BATTLE FOR BUTTLE": CANADA'S FIRST ENVIRONMENTAL CONFLICT

Buttle Lake is one of the most beautiful spots imaginable. The gloriously coloured profusion of lakes add to the attractiveness of the Park... bold promontories indent the shore-line, glacier-fed streams fall in picturesque waterfalls and cascades, their torrents forming delta fans, and primeval forests line the shores and clumps and single trees rest on precipitous cliffs and knife-like crags—the visitor wondering how they obtained a foothold—resemble inland lochs. The colourings vary and the shimmering surfaces reflect a great array of snowy peaks and glaciers. Buttle Lake has a tortuous shore-line, the bordering rock promontories—in places great cliffs towering 4,000 to 5,000 feet above the lake ... make wondrous scenery.

STRATHCONA PARK, VANCOUVER ISLAND
pamphlet from the BC Department of Lands, 1921

THE ROAD TO Buttle Lake that Roderick Haig-Brown and others had so long petitioned for was finally constructed in 1950, but not for the enjoyment of recreationists. Contrary to his hopes for a park to be enjoyed by all, instead his beloved Buttle Lake region became the focus of hydro-electric development in the context of postwar plans to increase power on Vancouver Island.

In realization of the potential of the Campbell River watershed first sighted by Mike King, the British Columbia Power Commission in the late 1940s began construction of a series of dams. To complete the project, the Power Commission hoped to construct the final dam at the Campbell River watershed source, Buttle Lake. The *Victoria Times* reported that the $568,000 Power Commission project would result in the lake level rising about forty to fifty feet. The agreement specified the Power Commission's construction of a public access road to Buttle Lake, and Baikie Bros. Logging won the contract. Harper Baikie, Wallace Baikie's brother and business partner, wrote that in any case, the Commission needed the road in order to access the proposed damsite.[1]

The Power Commission's intention to dam Buttle Lake would trigger one of Canada's first major environmental battles, spearheaded by Haig-Brown and Will Reid, the latter providing considerable financial resources to support their cause. Haig-Brown did not hesitate to express his views. He raised his concerns in newspapers and spoke out at numerous meetings. "Buttle Lake

TOP, LEFT Buttle Lake view. WILL J. REID FAMILY COLLECTION

TOP, RIGHT Shoreline of Buttle Lake in 1940s. WILL J. REID FAMILY COLLECTION

BOTTOM Penstocks from John Hart Lake to the generating station.
HEATHER HUGHSON

is the key point of Strathcona Park," he informed *Comox Argus* readers, "destroy it and you destroy the park."[2]

Haig-Brown and his supporters feared that rising water levels in Buttle would harm trout spawning grounds and change the flora of the lake, and suggested that damming Upper Campbell (the adjacent lake) would provide a magnificent lake for fishing purposes. Shoreline old growth forest would either be under water or would have to be logged, spoiling the original beauty and uniqueness of park scenery forever. "Buttle Lake," he declared, "is the most beautiful lake I have ever seen in my life."[3]

The debate that became known as the "Battle for Buttle" was to prove challenging and lengthy. It raged on for five years, and newspapers showcased the conflicting sides of the issue with diligence.[4] Despite the support Haig-Brown received from hunters' and anglers' groups, his friend Will Reid, and the outspoken Ruth Masters of the Comox Valley, who at that time was developing a reputation as an activist and protector of Strathcona Park,[5] he was up against formidable powers in government.

A series of hearings were held beginning August 8, 1951, to allow both sides to present their views to E.H. Tredcroft, the Comptroller of Water, and to question whether the project and its consequences had been thoroughly studied. This proved to be a forum for those who supported multiple use in parks and for conservationists, who came from a variety of organizations to support park values. In addition, the hearings raised long-standing issues about accessibility to the Park at the Buttle Lake entrance and about land use and ownership adjacent to the Park.

The Commission's first project in 1945 was to build a dam and generating system on the Campbell River at Elk Falls, even though the falls lay within a provincial park. Since the amended Forest Act of 1939 allowed for reduction of parks, the BC government, by a 1946 order-in-council, simply deleted about one hundred hectares from Elk Falls Park, and the falls were no longer protected from development. The public had no say in the matter; however, many were concerned that the once magnificent falls would be reduced

Wolf Creek. WILL J. REID FAMILY COLLECTION

to a mere trickle. Once the dam was constructed, the section of the Campbell River above the falls became a reservoir, and both this newly formed lake and the dam were named after the BC premier, John Hart. Three penstocks carried water to the generating station situated to the east of the Park.[6]

This did not bode well for Strathcona Park, forty-five kilometres west of Elk Falls, since the historical grand scheme for hydro-electric development included damming Buttle Lake, the source of the watershed.

The demand for power was expected to increase as the population of Vancouver Island grew, and at the same time as the John Hart development was proceeding, a licence was issued to create a reservoir at Lower Campbell Lake to store water there.[7] Application was also made for two more reservoirs—one at Upper Campbell Lake and one at Buttle Lake. In fact, the water rights to Buttle Lake, which included a main tributary, Wolf Creek, as well as the Elk River, had been acquired by the Power Commission several years earlier. In November 1940, by order-in-council under the Electric Power Act, permission was given with the proviso that requirements under the Water Act would be adhered to.[8] The Power Commission, however, wanted just one reservoir, at Buttle, and recognized that the Lieutenant-Governor-in-Council would have to give the Commission permission to dam the lake under the Strathcona Park Act.

In January of 1948, when at home in California, Reid received a letter from a friend in Victoria, Leigh Spencer, who suggested if Reid wished to learn more about the proposed dam project, he should visit John Hart, recently retired from his position as premier of British Columbia, who was having a period of rest in Santa Fe, California. That same month, Reid sent a copy of the letter to Haig-Brown, with whom he had begun corresponding in more familiar terms, addressing him as "Rod" as his friends did. Haig-Brown in turn, addressed Reid as "Will" or "Bill."

"Looks like it might be time," Reid wrote, "to start another campaign against the spoilers of your land, their methods, etc... to lick the loggers and save Buttle Lake I would join up with anybody."[9]

When Reid and Haig-Brown began their correspondence in the late 1930s, road and trail access to the lake was still an ongoing issue. A continual challenge was that the northeast side of Buttle Lake remained in the hands of private timber interests, and it was through this logged-off property that the public accessed the lake. The closest road to Buttle Lake came only as far as Upper Campbell Lake along a narrow single lane road, the original road put in from 1913 to 1915, and this road had not been maintained. Then a boat could be taken from Upper Campbell Lake to an overgrown trail and hence into Buttle by foot. An old railroad logging grade went as far as Buttle and, like many other grades, could have been converted to a road. Assistant Forester Trew, in his 1950 reconnaissance report, surmised that "several good logging roads in towards Buttle Lake and extension to the lake would not offer any great construction difficulties."[10]

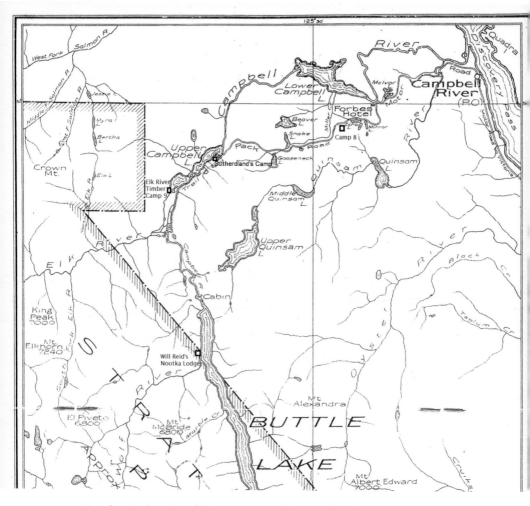

Map showing location of Camps 8 and 9, Sutherland's cabins and Reid cabins.

Importantly, the Parks Division was hesitant to develop the Buttle Lake corridor or improve access due to the BC Power Commission's proposed damsite. Flooding the lake would change the shoreline and obliterate any newly made trails or campsites.

To help mitigate access problems, Trew recommended a new boundary for the Park that would incorporate the section of Buttle Lake where the shores were in private hands, but he noted that there could be problems obtaining the remaining E & N lands and Elk River Timber Company holdings.

"The remaining E & N land fronting the north end of the lake (between Blocks 122-125)," he wrote, "should be acquired at an early date to prevent their alienation and the subsequent headaches to park administration." Nonetheless, it was felt that the number of people desiring access to Strathcona Park were few in number and "in the overall scheme of Provincial Park planning, developments in Strathcona Park hold a low priority."[11]

In April 1950, after Haig-Brown addressed the Campbell River Fish and Game Club on the attractions of the Park, the members asked the provincial Public Works Department to reopen the trail to Buttle Lake.[12]

Part of the concern felt by Haig-Brown and Reid was related to the BC Power Commission's handling of the Ladore damsite at Lower Campbell Lake. Work started at Ladore Falls, on the next dam to the west from Elk Falls, in 1949. Many locals were concerned that rising lake waters would disturb trout spawning grounds, and that trees not logged would create a hazard for boaters in the lake.[13] Reid mentioned in a letter to Haig-Brown dated March 9, 1950, that beginning in 1947, he had been conducting what he referred to as the "Lower Campbell Lake Clearing Fight."

Haig-Brown learned from meeting with George Melrose, Deputy Minister of Lands, and Cy Oldham, chief forester for the Parks Division, that the BC Power Commission had applied for Buttle Lake to become a reservoir. Fortunately, storage could not be granted without a public hearing. On the other hand, Reid and Haig-Brown were up against the 1927 ruling that allowed for the rise of water levels within a provincial park, the Power Commission's legal water rights, as well as the determination of the Power Commission to prove that Buttle Lake was an economically viable and ideal damsite.

There were further complications due to the fact that the proposed damsite was not within the boundaries of Strathcona Park;

TOP Old growth trees along Buttle Lake. WILL J. REID FAMILY COLLECTION

BOTTOM Beautiful view of Buttle Lake in 1936 with Mt McBride in the background. WILL J. REID FAMILY COLLECTION

only about three-quarters of the lake was within the Park. Nonetheless, damming, with its resultant rise in water levels, expected to be forty to fifty feet, would have a profound effect on the flora, fauna and appearance of the entire Buttle Lake area. In addition, all properties along the edge of the lake would be lost. To make matters worse, twenty-five million feet of timber would also be lost—irreplaceable old growth forest that would either be submerged underwater or would have to be logged and cleared prior to the resultant flooding.[14]

The Parks Division appeared to be washing its hands of the consequences of damming inside the Park, and Trew declared in his 1950 reconnaissance report that "the problem of dealing with the summer home owners, both trespassers and legal owners, should be worked out with the B.C. Power Commission."[15]

If the Trew report was an indication of the view held by officials in the Parks Division about the recreational value of the Buttle Lake area and Strathcona Park in general, then Reid and Haig-Brown were not likely to receive support from that quarter. Trew wrote:

> The park... was created on recommendation of a small interested group [and] has been reserved and retained since 1911 as a "Park" in the belief that it was of outstanding park value... It is very probably that the area, since set aside, gained a reputation by the mere fact that it was called a Park rather than on further investigation of its value.
>
> This latter point is important to note. It is a fact that has mislead public sentiment to a considerable degree throughout our brief park history and has been, and still is, source of much trouble in adequately administering over parks. Park values cannot readily be measured by any hard and fast yardstick such as is the case with timber and most other resources, but they can be appraised with some degree of common sense.[16]

Despite his disparaging remarks, Trew acknowledged that Buttle Lake was an area of "high attraction" and described the lake as beautiful, in an attractive setting:

> Its timbered shoreline drops off more or less steeply into the lake with gravel beaches at several of the river and creek deltas. The

lake, being long and narrow, is subject to occasional rough waters but is not particularly dangerous and there are a fair number of bays and coves for shelter. Fishing is said to be very good.[17]

A series of hearings was held, first in Courtenay and then in Victoria in 1953, to allow the public to have a voice and express its opposition or support of the project to Tredcroft, the Comptroller.

The Power Commission had engaged Mr. Davey as its solicitor to question the witnesses appearing before the Comptroller. Reid engaged Tom Norris, a lawyer who had extensive experience in presiding over Water Rights hearings, to represent him at the hearings.

"I appear on behalf of William J Reid… and Virginia Hancock Reid, now Virginia Hancock Moore," Norris told Tredcroft, "who have Crown granted mineral claims on the lake and who have useful and valuable properties on the lake… Mr. Reid's great objection, the objection of his daughter Mrs. Moore, is simply as international conservationists with all the other people whom I represent and who object." He went on to say:

Mr. Reid was educated in Edmonton, Alberta… Because of his outstanding work as a conservationist, a duck-producing area in Alberta has been called by the Government the Will J. Reid Area. In recognition of such work, he has been granted a lifetime hunting licence.

For twelve years he has devoted half his working hours to the work of Ducks Unlimited… was President for two years, and is now the California Chairman, and American Director of the Canadian Company. Mr. Leigh Stevenson MLA is also Director.

… Mr. Reid is anxious… to have preserved in all its beauty and majesty that magnificent lake with its scenery. He is apprehensive, and he feels, and he is quite sure, that the present application will destroy the value of that lake and the value of the park.[18]

Rail line from Elk River Timber Camp 9. WILL J. REID FAMILY COLLECTION

Alex McQuarrie, who represented the Auto Courts and Resorts Association of BC, felt it was important to clear up whose decision it should be to grant permission for damming. "In 1944," he said, "the government spent a large sum of money in acquiring timber licences to prevent the destruction of the beauty of the park, and the same occurred in 1929."

In his opinion, this was more than a decision about water rights, and the Comptroller was not the one to decide. The amendment in 1927 that allowed for the raising of water levels was a legislative decision, and this new decision should be dealt with with respect to the Park Act and decided by the Lieutenant Governor in council.[19]

One of the main arguments put forth by the Power Commission was that even with the expense of buying out those who had properties on the lake, the Buttle Lake site would cost quite a bit less than a damsite at Upper Campbell, where most of the land was privately owned, with the exception of two portions that abutted the lake that were still owned by the E & N. The Commission was prepared to pay Reid about $500,000 for his property. It also relied on Frederick Knewstubb's 1924 survey that recommended using Buttle Lake as a reservoir, even though it was pointed out that Knewstubb himself was against ruining the beauty of the lake. In addition, if Upper Campbell Lake were to be dammed instead, then Elk River Timber Company's railroad Camp 9, their rail lines and their road would be flooded out, and the lumber company would have to be compensated at an estimated cost of $1.67 million for the relocation of eleven miles of logging railway alone.[20]

The Sutherland brothers, who owned 3,400 acres of land estimated at a value of $6 per acre, would expect about $30,000. In 1951, the Baikie brothers had just Lot 846. The property belonging to Charlie Renecker was referred to as "a cedar swamp lying between Buttle and Upper Campbell—there is an owner of a cascara bark operation, and we have estimated compensation to him at $6000."[21] Before the lake was flooded, however, in about 1954, the Baikies had purchased Lot 1006 and the property from Renecker as an addition to their holdings around Upper Campbell, and the Power Commission would eventually be responsible for reimbursing Baikie Bros. Logging with a substantial settlement.[22]

With everything taken into consideration, the estimate for a dam at Upper Campbell put the cost at $1.6 million higher than for a dam at Buttle.[23] The Commission also emphasized that as a government body, it was not allowed to make a profit, and that its only interest was in serving the public, a key point, by catering to the growing demand for electric power on Vancouver Island.

The Commission engaged Acres & Company to make a new survey in 1945, and once again, Buttle Lake was recommended as a damsite. However, Dr. Victor Dolmage, a geologist who travelled to the lake in 1950, expressed doubts about the suitability of the proposed Buttle Lake site and recommended that nothing be done until engineers were able to drill, citing that it might be challenging to control seepage under the dam, and the dam itself might wash out because of sand.[24]

Numerous organizations and individuals came forward as witnesses to oppose the project. A heartfelt protest came from Mr. and Mrs. Jones, whose letter was read aloud at the August 15 hearing by Norris:

> We submit that the Power Commission, a publicly owned utility created by the duly elected representatives of the people of British Columbia, is assuming the role of a Frankensteinian monster attempting to destroy the heritage, the natural heritage of its creator, namely the electorate of the Province.
>
> The devastation already caused to one of the Island's most beautiful lakes, Lower Campbell Lake, by the progress of the Elk Falls power project, should give pause to the B.C. Power Commission in their mad haste to supply the bold buccaneers of industry with their insatiable demand for cheap power, power gained at the expense of our legally endowed public parklands, set apart for the benefit, advantage, and enjoyment of the people of British Columbia.[25]

The Director of Conservation in the Department of Lands and Forests, Mr. D.B. Turner, commented on the difficulty of allowing industrial interests to share Park resources.

> I must say that I do not subscribe very fully to the multiple use theory. Land use on Vancouver Island calls for very important decisions, particularly because of what might be termed the surging population. Vancouver Island has great material resources; it has great cultural and spiritual resources. We have to be very, very careful in choosing or in selecting what we do with our land.[26]

Roderick Haig-Brown spoke on behalf of the Affiliated Fish and Game Clubs of Vancouver Island, which represented the organized sportsmen of the Island and was affiliated with the BC Sportsmen's

Will Reid in the doorway of his cabin. WILL J. REID FAMILY COLLECTION

Council that represented the organized sportsmen of the entire province. He made it clear that the contents of his speech and the views, opinions and evidence expressed were fully supported at a regularly held meeting of the Affiliated Fish and Game Clubs.

> The affiliation feels first of all that this is a park area, deliberately set aside for recreational purposes, and that for this reason alone any interference whatsoever should be intensively examined. There is no other large public park area on Vancouver Island, and there can never be any other in a completely natural state.
>
> Since Strathcona Park is in a completely natural state, it is the only possible choice on Vancouver Island as a wilderness or primitive area, in the modern sense of park usage. The need for such areas has already been amply demonstrated by previous American and Canadian experience. Wherever such areas have been alienated from the public or damaged by industrial development their

loss has been very deeply felt, and much money has been spent in efforts to restore them.

A recreational area need not always be adversely affected by a dam; effects have sometimes been good, in that new or easier access has been provided and conditions for fish and wildlife have been improved. Full consideration has been given to these possibilities but in this instance they fail completely.

Buttle Lake already provides primary access to the main valleys of Strathcona Park, and any development of the park obviously depends on this; still more, it is clear that the high use area of the park will always be the lake itself. I say clear, it is clear as far as we can tell at this stage, one hundred years from now I might be wrong, but I think that is safe at this stage.[27]

Davey, the Power Commission's lawyer, did his best to malign Reid and to portray him as an unsuitable opponent of the development. He accepted that Reid had a mineral claim in the Park at lots 448 and 449 on the shores of Buttle Lake (under the name of his daughter Virginia), but cited passages from the Park Act that prohibited building personal accommodation in the Park. He referred to Reid as a "trespasser" who had no right to occupy his summer home within the Park, and alluded several times to the fact that only someone with an airplane could get into Buttle Lake. He also questioned why an American citizen who resided in California would become involved in this dispute and why this individual would use his status as president of Ducks Unlimited to lend strength to his position against development, when flooding of the lake was not going disturb bird habitat.

Reid was accused of misrepresenting the amount of support there was against dam construction, since one of the key supporters was his own caretaker, Harry Rogers. As well, it appeared that Reid had formed an organization, the Strathcona Park Association, as recently as 1951 that had questionable status as a conservation group.

In rebuttal, Reid's counsel, Norris, questioned Harvey E. Harris, Will Reid's long-time friend, a newspaper publisher, who stated that he was there to clarify Reid's interest in preserving Buttle Lake and the Park. Harris, a member of the BC Conservation League, said, "I have been heading the fight on the deal, opposing the damming in conjunction with the BC Natural Resources Conservation League, and came up to the area the first time in May 1942."

> At [that] time there was a move afoot to log off the lake down as far as Strathcona Park line, which is the north end of the lake... I succeeded in working out a proposition with the government who took over that timber, and also I worked out a proposition with the Elk River Timber company in which they left a fringe around the northern end of the lake.[28]

He went on to say that he had been up to the area fifteen or twenty times since 1942, and in that nine-year period he had been active in connection with Reid's views on Buttle Lake. Harris discussed his own relationship with the Conservation League, explaining that he assisted the president Mr. Stevens and Frank Bird of the Tourist Association, as well as a Mr. Baines of the Grosvenor hotel, who were "active in 1942 in saving Cathedral Grove to the Province of BC."[29] Harris was presently working with Roderick Haig-Brown and with Duncan Marshall who represented fish and game people. In addition, he was a friend to John Hart.[30]

Seeking further clarification, Norris stated: "Mr. Reid, as I understand it, is a great international conservationist?"

Harris responded that not only was Reid dedicated to Ducks Unlimited, and had helped with Cathedral Grove, but that "Reid has given large sums of money to the protection of redwoods in California."[31]

Harris also agreed with Norris that the value of the Park would be destroyed if flats and beaches of Buttle Lake were flooded. He verified that Reid paid $5,500 for his mineral claim, which came with three or four cabins, but that Reid was willing to lose his tenure if Strathcona was classified as Class "A" as he would like the area to be park for everyone. He went on to say that Reid "has had some 18 years here and I know that if the maintenance or whatever tenure he has now stands in the way of... preserving this park, then he is ready to walk out tomorrow."[32]

Despite all their best efforts and the expert handling of witnesses by Tom Norris, Water Rights Comptroller Tredcroft announced in early November of 1951 that he was giving the Power Commission the go-ahead to dam Buttle Lake. When pressed for reasons for his decision, he would only reveal in a letter to Norris dated November 15, 1951, that he did not feel park values would be destroyed by the water rising at Buttle Lake, and that his decision was "in the Public Interest."

Haig-Brown was quoted in a newspaper article saying that he did not see how from the hearings proceedings such a decision could be reached.[33]

Correspondence between Reid and Haig-Brown continued for several years after the hearings were over. In a November 18, 1951, letter to Reid, Haig-Brown talked about next steps, wondering what they should do. Conservationists were not giving up, and the premier, Byron Johnson, promised a debate in the Legislature for the coming year, but if conservationists were keen on launching an appeal, they had only thirty days in which to do so. Norris felt they should stand by their contention that the Comptroller had no jurisdiction in the Park. The head of the Power Commission, S.R. Weston, confirmed that nothing would go ahead until the situation was settled.

Reid was avidly following reports in Canadian newspapers from his home in Long Beach and told Haig-Brown in a November 23 letter that he was reaching out to supporters by telephone, as well as sending Harris to BC to keep him up to date. He assured Haig-Brown that "Tredcroft's decision didn't lower my morale one little bit!"

Reid was terribly disappointed, however, when W.A.C. Bennett was installed as the Social Credit premier of BC in 1952. Reid had been corresponding with Bennett while he was an Independent in the Legislature, and he had appeared to be on the side of conservationists. But now, as premier, he suddenly was extremely keen to see the power project come to fruition.[34] Time would show that Bennett was not above moving entire communities perceived to be in the way of progress in his zeal to electrify the westernmost province of Canada.[35] Reid referred to "Bennett's betrayal of a trust" in a letter to Haig-Brown and hoped that his decision to allow for the damming of Buttle would eventually cost him votes. "It's a pretty tough break," he wrote, "—but the fight isn't over!"

In Reid's letters to Haig-Brown during this period, he was critical of Crown Zellerbach and their plans to develop Campbell River by way of establishing a pulp and paper mill; however his sentiments were at odds with those of townsfolk who were excited about the prospect of growth and prosperity signalled by the creation of the Zellerbach mill. The economic benefit to the community in many individuals' eyes far outweighed the environmental cost of creating power.

Bennett's support of the power project corresponded with the Island Chambers of Commerce also suddenly withdrawing their support of conservationists and with the opening of the Elk Falls (Crown Zellerbach) pulp and paper mill at Duncan Bay, just north of Campbell River. Campbell River had only been incorporated as a village in 1948—before that, the settlement was considered to be an organized territory under control of the province.[36] Campbell River was gaining a new identity in the wake of this new era of economic growth and job stability; it was becoming a settled community, "not just the logger's Saturday night town it used to be."[37]

More than 1,000 men had been employed to build the mill, which was facilitated by the completion of the John Hart and Ladore dam projects, and the village reaped the benefit of the influx of workers as "new investor money poured into the area as hotels, landlords, beer parlours and cafes did a landslide business."[38] Bennett, who attended the grand opening of the mill, was quoted as saying that the Duncan Bay mill development (Elk Falls Mill) represented "free enterprise at its best."[39]

Many of the construction workers were offered jobs at the mill, and families moved to Campbell River from Ocean Falls, where the

mill was scheduled for closure. Within a couple of years the population of Campbell River doubled to 2,600, with a sixth of that
being school-aged children, prompting the construction of three
new elementary schools, a grocery franchise, a new church and
community hall, followed by a hospital. By 1958 the mill employed
about 500.

With the state of buoyancy of Campbell River citizens, it was a
hard sell to halt what was deemed progress, although a few stalwart
conservation groups, such as the Conservation League, continued
to lobby for at least a reconsideration of moving the damsite to
Upper Campbell Lake.

Later, there would be other environmental costs associated
with the mill in terms of pollution in both the air and water, yet
many owed their living to the mill, and the mill gave back to the
community. In resource rich British Columbia, job creation and
stability would often result in an uneasy blend of prosperity and
environmental degradation.

Reid continued to be critical of Crown Zellerbach, contending
in his letters that there had to be some form of collusion between
Bennett, Zellerbach and the Power Commission. He believed that
Zellerbach paid for Bennett's election campaign and would be the
recipient of Buttle Lake timber, as the trees around the perimeter
of the lake were cleared through an agreement with the Power
Commission, which was responsible for disposal of the timber.
Reid's suspicions appeared confirmed when his caretaker at Nootka
Lodge reported that clearing had begun in 1955 and a mill employee
he knew referred to Buttle Lake timber arriving at the mill.

Reid also believed Baikie Bros. Logging must have the Minister of Forests in their pocket, since they had acquired some of
the former E & N lands around the lake that had previously been
owned by Elk River Timber. "How endless the Battle seems," he
wrote in 1953.

Correspondence between Reid and Haig-Brown frequently
touched on the subject of how the clearing of trees would be handled, and both were concerned that if the Power Commission was

successful in its request for an amendment to the existing water rights licence, then wood debris and stumpage would be left at the lake.

Newspapers continued to report at various intervals from 1952 to 1954 that the project was stalled. Harper Baikie later recalled that test drilling at Buttle Lake revealed the ground formation to be unsuitable.[40]

Reid received reports on the drilling, and he heard in early 1954 that an expert predicted a dam at the foot of Buttle Lake would not hold water. Now, despite the Power Commission's initial declaration that a dam at Upper Campbell Lake would be difficult to build and twice as expensive as constructing at Buttle Lake, they were forced to move the site away from Buttle. By May, drillers were ordered to move to Upper Campbell Lake. With the likelihood that Upper Campbell Lake would be the location of a new damsite, Haig-Brown and Reid discussed how high water levels might still rise in Buttle Lake, and hoped that it wouldn't be more than seven feet, thus preserving timber, buildings and spawning grounds. Reid wrote on August 19, 1955, "Obviously they plan to raise the lake 18 ft above high water."

Once the Commission accepted that Upper Campbell was the better choice, it capitulated to Haig-Brown's proviso that the Campbell River and adjacent Upper Campbell Lake valleys be logged and cleared to avoid the problem with debris that had been experienced in Lower Campbell Lake. Much of the property to be cleared belonged to Baikie Bros. Logging, consisting of a strip approximately six miles long and half a mile wide bordering Upper Campbell Lake and the Upper Campbell River toward Buttle Lake.[41]

Damming Upper Campbell may have mitigated the damage to the Buttle Lake basin, but the stunning old growth trees dotting Buttle's shoreline would have to be cleared, since the lake was expected to rise about seventeen feet, as predicted by Reid. Ultimately, the level of Upper Campbell was expected to rise 137 feet, creating "one hell of a big area to be flooded," Harper Baikie recalled, and Baikie Bros. were assigned to clear 1,600 acres of

View of Upper Campbell Lake looking south into Park prior to flooding.

the total area. Myrna Boulding believed that her father, Wallace, and his brothers were in favour of the dam construction, and thus on the opposite side of the debate from Haig-Brown. But Harper Baikie reflects that while Myrna and "everyone in Campbell River" may have thought so, the Baikies lost a large portion of their future log supply, putting them "in a very bad situation." Moreover, they had to invest in additional equipment and hire more workers, and because the lake level rose more quickly than anticipated, they worked under enormous pressure. In the end, Baikie insists they were not adequately compensated for their timber, their labour or their financial investment, and were, in fact, victims of expropriation.[42]

While the Baikie brothers contended with the physical and financial challenges imposed on them by the flooding, Haig-Brown suffered an emotional loss. Not only would the lake he loved be

Strathcona Dam under construction. MYRNA BOULDING COLLECTION

altered irrevocably and forever, but in April 1956 he received the
sad news that Will Reid had passed away. Reid's family felt that the
battle had drained him, and that perhaps it was fortunate he did
not live to see the devastation around his beloved Buttle Lake as
trees were first logged, then towed away. In the end the Reid family
was never compensated for the loss of their property.

Haig-Brown's daughter Mary remembered that Myrna Boulding congratulated her father on winning the "Battle," but in fact
Haig-Brown felt defeated and saw no reason to celebrate. He was
depressed for about a year afterward.[43]

Work began on what would be named the Strathcona Dam at
the northeast side of Upper Campbell Lake in 1956, and in 1958,
when the valley was flooded, Buttle Lake as predicted rose by
about five metres. The entire valley stretching from Upper Campbell Lake through the Upper Campbell River to Buttle Lake was
irreversibly changed, and even today, stumps from trees that
were felled during the clearing still litter the beaches. Before the

flooding was to occur, Reid flew Haig-Brown and his family over the Park and Buttle Lake so they could all see for one last time the unspoiled vista. Haig-Brown pointed out favourite beaches, picnic spots and fishing locales that he said would be gone forever.[44]

The first major battle was over, but less than ten years later another industry would eye the south end of Buttle Lake, and the ensuing threat that mining posed to the lake's ecology plunged Strathcona Park into further conflict.

At the same time, Comox Valley residents, after many years of lobbying, received the good news that a decision had been made to add the highly desirable Forbidden Plateau to the Park. Situated on the eastern boundary of Strathcona Park, the Plateau had been known for decades as a popular destination for hikers and skiers, who contributed an extraordinary number of volunteer hours to making trails and signs and building cabins for the use of outdoor enthusiasts on private land owned by the CPR. Forbidden Plateau would now enjoy the status of provincial park land.

FORBIDDEN PLATEAU

Strathcona Park, an alpine area with unrivalled beauty set in the central portion of Vancouver Island, offers much to those who seek an outdoor vacation. It is not a well-groomed park; here nature is found in primeval beauty. Snow-topped peaks and glaciers await the skill of the mountaineer; the angler can find streams and lakes teeming with trout; nature-lover, photographer, or artist, wondrous vistas of alpine scenery; and all who enjoy the great outdoors will find here an ideal place for a summer vacation.

STRATHCONA PARK, VANCOUVER ISLAND
pamphlet from the BC Department of Lands, 1921

With no natural boundaries, Forbidden Plateau appears on a map as a curiously shaped appendage on the east side of Strathcona Park. The idea that it should be set aside as park land occurred to its promoters very early in the twentieth century, but it did not achieve this status until 1967, when it was added to the already existing Strathcona Provincial Park. The Plateau, with its beautiful vistas, numerous trails, mountain peaks, lakes and slopes, has long been a favourite recreational destination for hikers and skiers, and this focus on recreational development rather than industrial development has resulted in a history that differs significantly from that of the Buttle Lake corridor.

Prospectors once roamed the Plateau, but there were never any "lucky strikes" to draw mineral development or even placer miners. Logging took place in and around the area but ceased once the boundaries defining park land were established.

In addition to its curious shape, this upland bears a curious misnomer, as the area is neither forbidden nor a plateau. In his 1950 *Reconnaissance Report*, Trew notes that it

> is actually a levelling off of the upland slopes flanking the Coast Ranges. It is in no way plateau-like or level, but is studded with knolls and ridges and broken up further by canyons and cliffs. It is high enough to be sub-alpine and is dotted with a multitude of small lakes with clear mirroring waters.[1]

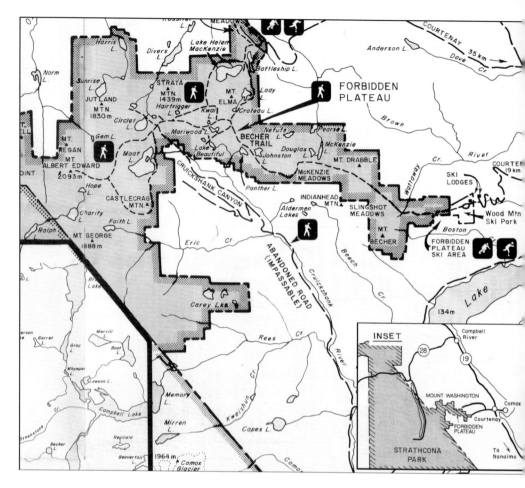

ABOVE Map showing Forbidden Plateau addition to Strathcona Park. STRATH-
CONA PROVINICIAL PARK, BC PARKS MINISTRY OF ENVIRONMENT AND PARKS 1987

OPPOSITE There are many small lakes and tarns at Forbidden Plateau. BETTY
BROOKS COLLECTION

The area elevated to about 1,200 metres can be described as
roughly being bordered by three mountains: on the northeast by
Mt Washington, on the northwest by Mt Becher and on the west
by Mt Albert Edward, with Mts Indian Head, George, Regan, Jutland and Drabble along the outer perimeter. Betty Brooks, in her
1989 report for BC Parks, notes that while this description fits what
most local people would consider the Plateau area, "the official

lines on the most recent map, vary from the traditional notion considerably."[2]

The Comox Glacier, which is just to the south of Forbidden Plateau within Strathcona Park boundaries, "is isolated from the rest of the park by deep valleys, canyons, and generally rough mountain

TOP Comox Glacier. BETTY BROOKS COLLECTION

BOTTOM K'omoks Village, circa 1910. IMAGE 989.96.4 COURTESY OF THE
COURTENAY AND DISTRICT MUSEUM

country. The recognized route is by trail from the Puntledge River
at the north end of Comox Lake and up along the eastern divide
of Red Pillar Creek."[3]

When the Spanish explorers Francisco de Eliza and José Maria Nárvaez left the fort of San Miguel at Nootka Sound and sailed around the southern tip of Vancouver Island and up the east side as far as present day Comox in 1791, they would have easily sighted the Comox Glacier from their ships. Their interest ended at surveying the coast, and they recorded their findings in a wonderful map of 1791 that shows Vancouver Island as a peninsula attached to the British Columbia mainland.

The K'omoks First Nation, who for centuries had inhabited the coast, would have been well acquainted with what the interior mountains could offer, but they did not have to travel far inland to hunt for elk, deer or bear or to forage for berries. According to Reginald Pidcock in his diary begun in the late 1860s, wildlife grazed and berries grew along the Tsolum and Puntledge Rivers at low elevations. He recorded that the peaceful coastal peoples had suffered from raids from Interior Alberni Nations, the Schasahts (Tse-shahts) and Opetchesahts (Hupacasaths), and were reluctant to venture inland.[4] There is, however, an interesting story from the Moon family about finding gold in the hills:

Mrs. Moon had an ancestor by the name of Hoomtie, he was a fine hunter and ventured far in quest of game. While Hoomtie was out hunting for elk on the hills we call Forbidden Plateau he became thirsty. In seeking water he came across a small hole in the rocks from which bubbled up a lively spring. Hoomtie laid aside his bow and arrows and knelt to refresh himself. To his surprise the water seemed to glitter. Very odd, thought the hunter as he looked upon it with pleasure yet quite unaware as to what he had discovered. Years passed. Hoomtie had grown old when white men first came to Comox Valley. He soon learned of their desire for the yellow stuff called gold. Gold was valuable. The old man knew at last what it was he had seen at the bubbling hole high in the hills. Hoomtie could never undertake the strenuous journey in search of the golden spring he had found long years ago but his son-in-law and nephew were strong young men, they

TOP Cruickshank Canyon. BETTY BROOKS COLLECTION

BOTTOM Mount Albert Edward. JOE MCCARTHY

must go in his place. These two were given as detailed a description of the area and the route to travel as the old hunter could recall. Together they set forth, only to return empty-handed. Time and time again the young men scoured the hills but never a sign of the glittering spring could they find. Hoomtie lived to be 100, hoping and hoping his tribesmen would come upon the hole in the rocks where glittering water gushed forth but all in vain. It has never been found to this day.[5]

By 1862, a group of thirty settlers, encouraged by Vancouver Island's governor James Douglas, descended upon the Comox Valley, arriving on the gunboat HMS *Grappler* from Victoria. Immigrants from Great Britain and Canada's maritime provinces followed, boosting the white population of the district to 134 by 1868. First arrivals recorded that there were two small villages of K'omoks People, whose population had been decimated by war and disease.[6]

Dr. Robert Brown, a member of the Royal Geographic Society, is credited with conducting the first survey of the central interior of Vancouver Island; in 1864 he headed up an expedition out of Victoria. John Buttle was a member of this party. The surveyors penetrated into the interior via the Brown and Puntledge Rivers, and came upon Comox Lake.[7] Here they took note of a river they named the Cruickshank River, that finds its origins in the snows of the Plateau, then winds its way through the steep sides of Cruickshank Canyon before emptying into the lake. Their discovery of coal in the Brown River led to the development of coal mining in Cumberland.[8]

The Esquimalt and Nanaimo Railway Company obtained the whole of the Forbidden Plateau area in its original land grant back in the late 1800s. Yet the fact that the Plateau was situated on private land did not deter outdoor enthusiasts, trappers and prospectors from entering the area. Later in the 1920s, a prospector named John Brown, who worked in the Cumberland coal mines, became familiar with the terrain while searching for minerals in the Plateau area. Tom Anderson, a trapper in those same years, explored the region and built a number of cabins on the Plateau.[9] Others made forays into the upland; however, the area's beauty was not well advertised until the City of Courtenay was looking for a way to increase its water supply, and exploration commenced to find a lake suitable for damming.

The city received its water supply via the Brown River, and Clinton Wood, who was then engineer for the City of Courtenay, embarked on a trip in 1925 to find the source of the river. He followed a miner's trail toward Mt Becher, and along the way encountered John Brown, who took him to several lakes, but they were unsuccessful in determining where the river began. The following year, Wood, accompanied by Cecil "Cougar" Smith, an experienced woodsman and trapper, explored more of the Plateau, including Mt Albert Edward. As a consequence of Wood's explorations, it was determined that Goose Lake (later named McKenzie) would be dammed and a reservoir created.[10]

The power of the press, at a time when people avidly read newspapers, played an important role in getting the word out about the Plateau.

"So impressed was I however, " wrote Wood, "by the great beauty of the new land which I had seen for the first time... and the possibility of having it developed into a great playground for the people of British Columbia, Canada and our visitors, that I could not resist writing a short article in the *Comox Argus*."[11] The newspaper's editor, Ben Hughes, was intrigued, particularly with Wood's notion that the region should be used as a "provincial playground."

Hughes and Wood collaborated on several articles about the Plateau, and Hughes came up with an imaginary "Indian Legend," which Betty Brooks wryly notes was "manufactured out of whole cloth."[12] The legend was published in the Vancouver *Daily Province* in 1925, garnering widespread attention. It told a story of how the K'omoks People, when concerned about raids from nearby tribes, would hide their women and children on the plateau. Apparently after returning from a particular raid, the men went to the plateau to retrieve the women and children but they were not there.

Betty Brooks at the Comox District Mountaineering Club cabin at Mt Becher.

All that was found was red lichen on the snow, resembling blood. Perhaps evil spirits were responsible or a hairy beast later called Sasquatch; in any case, according to the legend, the area was avoided by the K'omoks after that.[13]

Comox Valley youth, some just one generation removed from those who were pioneers of the region, were clearly imbued with the spirit of adventure passed down to them by their forebears. They joined the Comox District Mountaineering Club, which had been formed by Wood, the first president, and four directors on November 4, 1927. Geoffrey Capes was a director and was influential in promoting the region.[14] The club had a small but active membership that organized summer camps, constructed a cabin at Mt Becher and wrote letters to the provincial government requesting park status. With no Parks Branch to assist them, they built trails and made directional signs.[15]

Clinton Wood on Mt Becher, January 1929. Geoff Capes photo. IMAGE P225-273
COURTESY OF THE COURTENAY AND DISTRICT MUSEUM

In order to do this, the club required permission from the Canadian Pacific Railway, which had purchased that section of the E & N land grant from James Dunsmuir in 1905. The CPR, through negotiations with Wood, allowed citizens to use the area, but at the time was no interested in selling it to any governments so that it could be set aside as park land.[16]

A further draw to the area would be fishing. Unlike Buttle Lake and the Elk River Valley, the Forbidden Plateau waters did not boast a natural trout population. In 1929, a shipment of 100,000 Kamloops trout eggs from the Department of Fisheries were sent to Courtenay by train. Wood described the challenges of transporting this precious cargo over the trails by horse in hot summer weather, as they had to keep the eggs cool enough that they wouldn't hatch prematurely.

"Pack horses, packers, food, blankets, tents and all miscellaneous articles," he wrote, "which would be required for at least a week entirely out of touch with civilization for a party of at least 10 persons and oats for at least three pack horses had to be arranged for."[17]

At one point the horses had to swim across a river, with the supplies transported over a swaying cable suspension bridge to reach the trail head. There they waited until a truck delivered the eggs that had been picked up from the train.

The going was tricky and often hazardous as they reached higher elevations heading up to McKenzie Lake, and horses frequently lost their footing along the slippery snow path. The group attained the lake and found a "gravelly-bottomed stream" flowing into it that was ideal for planting eggs. They carried on to even higher terrain, with a few mishaps involving the horses along the way, and made it to Panther Lake. They deposited more eggs, then deciding that with no pasture for the horses and only more snow ahead, it was wisest to turn around.

In 1930 and 1931, Wood's son Stuart, accompanied by a Captain Beadnell, would stock sixteen more lakes. And in 1932, Wood cast a fly into McKenzie Lake. "A swirl of water, a singing reel, and a few minutes later a three pound trout panting on shore was the visible proof of the success of the strenuous venture in 1929."[18]

His many excursions into the Plateau led Wood in 1928 to consider looking for an easier way in, rather than by way of the Becher and Brown trails. He organized a party to explore the possibility of entering the Plateau via Dove Creek, and found this to be a big improvement. On their explorations the party came upon a beautiful alpine meadow they named Paradise Meadows, and for the first time saw Battleship Lake. The trail was officially opened by Lieutenant-Governor Randolph Bruce on July 17, 1929. Until it was obliterated by logging in the 1960s, the trail proved a popular access to the subalpine.[19]

Comox District Mountaineering Club (CDMC) members had already begun construction on their cabin at Mt Becher, after selecting a spot in May of 1928 that provided a view of Boston Lake, Comox Lake, Comox Spit and most of the valley, and had a small tarn nearby as well as a creek. The intrepid and determined members would haul building material up to the spot, and within a year the cabin was "fit for use."[20] The addition of bunks meant users could stay overnight, and basic dry goods such as flour, salt and pepper were left in the cabin. From here, locals could ski and go tobogganing, and on weekends there were sometimes as many as twenty-five staying in the cozy building.[21] "The snow was usually so deep," wrote Brooks, "one had to dig down to the door to gain entrance."[22] She also noted that often the entire cabin would be covered in snow, and users had to know in which tree they would find the snow shovel hanging. Betty Brooks (née Hatfield) was a long-time member of the CDMC and would later attend the University of Victoria to study biology. In the 1960s, while a student, she worked for three summer seasons at BC Parks' Miracle Beach office and became the first female park naturalist to work in the provincial park system.[23]

Another camp open to the public was at Croteau Lake. For those who wished to climb nearby mountains such as Mt Albert Edward, the Croteau Camp provided a base and was accessed either by hiking the Dove Creek trail or via horseback.[24] Eugene Croteau, an outfitter, established the camp with two large cabins—one a cookhouse with all the basic necessities, situated at the edge

TOP View from Mt Becher looking at Island range. BETTY BROOKS COLLECTION

BOTTOM Betty Cox on horseback at Croteau Lake. BETTY BROOKS COLLECTION

of the lake; the other, a sleeping cabin, higher up. Guests would often stay for a week.

Croteau was born in Quebec and came west when a teenager. He learned about the hospitality business while working at the Guichon Hotel in Vancouver, beginning in 1894, where he met

TOP Eugene Croteau taking his tea tray to guests, 1943. Lynn Hilton photo. FROM "HISTORY OF FORBIDDEN PLATEAU," COMPILED BY RUTH MASTERS AT THE COURTENAY AND DISTRICT MUSEUM

BOTTOM Upper sleeping cabin at Croteau camp. BETTY BROOKS COLLECTION

Croteau Lake showing main cabin in 1949. BETTY BROOKS COLLECTION

such luminaries as Richard McBride. By 1917 he had found his way to the Comox Valley, and in the late 1920s, built his camp. In addition to the main sleeping cabin, he added six tents with wooden floors. "In the first year of operations," wrote local mountaineer and historian Lindsay Elms, "nearly two hundred people had stayed and passed through his camp and by the end of 1932 that figure rose to well over two hundred."[25]

In 1939, Ruth Masters worked at the camp for a season as a cook and guided hikers on some of the easier trails. She had first visited the Plateau six years earlier with Geoffrey Capes and joined the Comox District Mountaineering Club in 1938. In September 1939, visitors coming up on a pack train brought the news that war had broken out in Europe.

Croteau had a reputation for knowing how to treat his guests well and for entertaining them with stories. After he retired in the

Snow at the top of Mt Becher. BETTY BROOKS COLLECTION

mid-1940s, he left the camp open to whoever wanted to use it. While nothing of the original camp, except for some foundation logs, was left on the spot, Brooks has remarked that "the spirit of 'Croteau of the Plateau' is still there to greet the visitor."[26]

Throughout the 1930s, members of the CDMC tirelessly promoted the Plateau and performed the upkeep on the trails, and they were rewarded with increased popularity of the upland for fishing, hiking and, later, skiing.

It was during this time that Clinton Wood thought that if he could impress the vice-president of the CPR with the idea that the Plateau was a ski mecca, the company might "turn [the land] over to the province for a park. No one had as yet skied there, but not to be daunted, [he] got hold of a pair of skis, put them on, and took a picture of himself. He had to stay up until 4 a.m. to process the film and get a blow-up done in time."[27]

In the early 1930s, Wood was able to purchase a few small plots of land from the CPR with the intention of building a large lodge near the entrance to the Plateau area, and to build smaller cabins at some other favourite locations. When tracks were removed from a railway grade that had extended up to the 2,000-foot level, this provided the basis for a road. By 1934, the road was passable with a motor vehicle. At this point, Wood retired from his position with the city, and his entire family moved up to their new location to focus all their time and energy on the new endeavour.

After a month they had only two rough cabins and tents for accommodation, but they already had guests from Victoria. Despite having to obtain water from a creek, and having no refrigeration, Mary Wood managed to serve tea and cook meals, and "the guests were delighted."[28]

Their older boy, Stuart, enjoyed summers guiding guests throughout the Plateau, and the younger son, Gavin, was assisting by the time he was five. The Second World War changed this challenging but idyllic life when Stuart, who had gone to fight overseas, was killed in Cologne in a bombing raid in 1943.

The Woods sold the lodge and moved to Campbell River, but kept a cabin on Moat Lake, where they spent summer holidays. Mariwood Lake is named for Mrs. Wood.[29]

In 1946, the Plateau was the epicentre for the largest earthquake recorded in Canadian history, measuring 7.3 on the Richter scale. There was not much damage in the immediate area, but it was recorded that nearly all of the chimneys in Cumberland crumbled on that day.[30]

Forbidden Plateau Lodge with Courtenay Lookout in background, sketch by Edward Goodal, 1946. BETTY BROOKS COLLECTION

In the meantime, Clinton Wood, along with many members of the community and the CDMC continued to lobby both the government for park status for the Plateau and the CPR for its land.

When members of the Courtenay–Comox Board of Trade joined members of the Cumberland Board for a meeting in 1930, a topic on the agenda was how to convince "certain powerful interests [to] look... with favour on a National Park site on the West Coast."[31] The idea was that both Strathcona Park and Forbidden Plateau, as well as Long Beach on the west coast of the Island, should be park land, offering together mountains, subalpine and oceanfront. To that end the Boards of Trade formed a Parks Committee that would work with the Courtenay Parks Board.

The *Comox Argus* continued to publish articles regarding the desired designation throughout the 1930s and '40s, including discussions about potential rights to natural resources such as minerals, timber and water.[32] It also noted that "the board has been carrying on for years to get the provincial government to turn over Strathcona Park to the Dominion government as a national park."[33]

Chess Lyons of the Parks Division was engaged in a reconnaissance of the Plateau in the late 1940s when he was asked to assist a filmmaker. He was "quite captivated by the place."[34] He met Clinton Wood while there who had his ski operation. Wood was still lobbying for the Plateau to become park land, and Lyons also felt as a result of his visit that it should be preserved and included this in his report. Lyons' report prompted Mickey Trew, also of the Parks Division, who was aware of the public's desire to see Forbidden Plateau become park land, to recommend adding the Plateau to Strathcona Park:

> The Forbidden Plateau would be by far the most popular part of the amalgamated Strathcona Park. It would be possible to expand this popularity over to Buttle Lake and make better use of that area. Thus, with a resort centre on the Plateau, it would add to a holiday stay there to be able to trail ride down to a resort centre on Buttle Lake for a change in scenery, setting and recreational activities... In addition, it would allow an organized circuit trip with varied means of transportation and recreation.[35]

Trew listed the CPR's conditions for turning the land over to the province:

> 1. That no marketable timber be included in this area, or that provision be made for its eventual disposal by the company or acquisition by the Government

> 2. That all mineral rights be retained by the company.

> 3. That at least a road or some equivalent form of development be undertaken before the company completes the transfer.[36]

Trew felt that there was no marketable timber; neither did he believe that mining would conflict in any "untenable or uncompromising manner with recreational uses."[37] He also envisioned a rail line that would transport visitors up the Plateau, putting the new Park on the same footing as Manning and Garibaldi Parks.

On April 29, 1953, the *Argus* ran an article that concurred with Trew's vision.

Plateau and Buttle Lake

The Associated Chambers of Commerce on Vancouver Island and the Courtenay District Fish and Game Protective Association suggested immediate action be taken to include Forbidden Plateau and adjoining areas into Strathcona Park, believing the Plateau area had "tremendous potential as both a Summer and Winter tourist resort comparable to other famous mountain resorts and unequaled on Vancouver Island."[38]

On August 20, 1958, the *Argus* published a hopeful article stating that a survey was being conducted by the Department of Recreation and Conservation, perhaps in consideration of including the Plateau in Strathcona Park.[39] Although it took another nine years, in May 1967 the land was acquired from the CPR, and Forbidden Plateau was at last made part of Strathcona Park. The Plateau's recreational popularity, however, was unrelated to its park status, and trails, cabins, signage and activities were the result of hard and consistent voluntary work by local citizens and the Comox District Mountaineering Club.

Ruth Masters played an active role with the CDMC for over fifty years, working as secretary and actively taking part in producing hand painted signage, and building and improving trails. Masters worked for forty years as a legal secretary in Courtenay and spent her free time attending protests, hiking and contributing to local history. She gained a reputation as an outspoken environmentalist and was a self-styled staunch protector of parks, wilderness and wildlife. Her true appreciation of how precious Canada was began

TOP, LEFT Betty and friends hiking on the way to Mt Becher ski hill. BETTY
BROOKS COLLECTION

TOP, RIGHT Forbidden Plateau Lodge in deep snow. BETTY BROOKS COLLECTION

BOTTOM, LEFT Betty and friends on a ski outing in front of Forbidden
Plateau Lodge. BETTY BROOKS COLLECTION

BOTTOM, RIGHT Fallen skiers BETTY BROOKS COLLECTION

when she served in London, England, during the war years and
could see her country from a distance. Then in the 1950s, when
it looked as if Buttle Lake might be dammed, she was compelled
to join in the Battle for Buttle with Roderick Haig-Brown as she

A ski trail through the snow on Mt Becher. BETTY BROOKS COLLECTION

considered the value of Strathcona Park's lakes, mountains and forests that she had enjoyed for many years.[40] She passed away in 2017, at the age of ninety-seven.

Throughout the 1930s, '40s and '50s, skiing was a popular form of recreation in the Comox Valley at Forbidden Plateau, and this continued into the '90s. The CDMC was involved in building a ski tow at the Forbidden Plateau ski hill after the Second World War.[41] "By the early 1950s, members maintained a run from the Mount Becher cabin, through the forest, to the logged-off slope above Forbidden Plateau Lodge and built an additional cabin along the way as a stopping point."[42]

Betty Brooks and her friends enjoyed both downhill and cross-country skiing at Mt Becher, where there was a run from the Mt Becher cabin down to Forbidden Plateau Lodge. Brooks said if the snow was deep enough, they would even ski right off the roof of the Lodge.[43]

The destination grew in popularity as more amenities were added, and the operators, the Mt Becher Ski Development Society, put in a T-bar, followed in 1972 by the first chairlift on Vancouver Island. By the 1980s, however, snowfall was no longer consistent and the hill was no longer lucrative. Then, sadly, the Forbidden Plateau Lodge burned down in July 1982. By 1999 a day lodge built by the Society collapsed under heavy snow.

The nearby Mt Washington ski resort was already in development by 1979, and two chairlifts were added there in 1984. With its accommodation, higher elevation and consistent conditions, the resort soon took over as the Island's main ski destination. Forbidden Plateau ski hill closed for good in 2002.[44]

Although there is no more skiing at the Plateau, the area has continued to attract outdoor enthusiasts. In order to better accommodate those who have wished to access and stay at the more remote locations on Forbidden Plateau, BC Parks in 2017 began work on wilderness accommodation at the old Croteau site, completed in 2019. A large yurt and twelve tent pads were constructed for overnight sleeping, and composting toilet facilities were installed. A small dock was put in on Croteau Lake. Strathcona Park Area Supervisor Andy Smith explained that the Croteau Lake group site was built with donations and grant money as well as BC Parks funds. It is unique, being the only backcountry site that can be reserved, and has proved to be very popular.[45]

A MINE IN A PARK?

The chief impression found on a trip into Strathcona Park is one of amazement … The Park abounds in all the attributes of nature in its primeval condition; giant forests; sunlit lakes bounded by bold rock shapes and overshadowed by snowy peaks and glaciers reflected in their placid, sunlit, vari-coloured waters; … lofty spires—Nature's great cathedrals; lace falls leaping from white, pale-blue, and green glaciers; little lakes of blue and green and turquoise that sparkle like jewels set in a velvet, some lying above the timber-line in brown rock basins trimmed with heather and gay-hued alpine flora to the edge of the eternal snows reaching down close to them.

STRATHCONA PARK, VANCOUVER ISLAND
pamphlet from the BC Department of Lands, 1921

CONFUSION OVER the role of parks and their use would only increase in the 1960s. In 1957, after the Buttle episode was over with, the provincial government created the Ministry of Recreation and Conservation, perpetuating the park classification system and repealing the 1911 Strathcona Park Act. While on one hand, capital development in parks was funded and the heritage site Barkerville created, on the other, portions of three provincial parks had been flooded, and logging tenures had been issued. In other words, in existing parks, lands could be traded with timber companies eager to access stands within parks and willing to give up less lucrative property.

In addition, in 1964, W.A.C. Bennet approved an order-in-council to permit mineral claim staking in Class A and B parks larger than two thousand hectares. Strathcona Park fell into this category.[1]

The Park Act of 1965 did little to mitigate the damage that was about to be done. Even though the Act stated that parks were created for the purpose of conservation, with the explanation that conservation meant preserving parks as natural environments "for inspiration, use and enjoyment of the public,"[2] the public was expected to give up portions of these natural environments for industrial use. This came at a time when parks had clearly become important in the province, with annual attendance at five million.[3]

New designations were created labelled "Nature Conservancy" and "Recreation Area." Within Nature Conservancies, areas of scenic, flora and fauna value were unquestionably protected; however, Recreation Area status would cause confusion.

The Park Act was to provide a legal framework within which to manage parks, with the intention that nature-based recreation was the purpose of parks. At the time, it was recognized that a minister should be appointed to oversee and make decisions about parks. This did not mean that an appointed minister would or had to uphold a conservation policy for all parks. In fact, an unfortunate proviso in the Act, open to abuse by politicians, stated that the "removal, destruction, disturbance, damaging or exploitation of natural resources in parks" was permitted if the minister so wished. In the event that a Class A park was still not open to development, all or part of it could be reclassified to Class B.[4]

In what seems to have been a carefully orchestrated plan, after becoming Minister of Recreation in 1964, former Minister of Mines Kenneth Kiernan made changes to Strathcona Park status by an order-in-council that, on the surface, appeared to favour recreational values. In reality, these changes paved the way for Western Mines to develop its claims.

Western Mines' claims dated back to 1918, and some other mining claims pre-dated the formation of the park. Although the provincial government made intermittent attempts to buy out these claims, the process was never completed; some were honoured by certain provisions, as were some timber licences, even though Strathcona was a Class A park. The classification system should have cleared up misunderstandings about how park land should be used, since neither mining nor commercial logging was allowed in Class A parks, but for Strathcona, Class A status did little to protect park values.[5] When Western Mines Ltd. first outlined plans to situate an open-pit mine at the south end of Buttle Lake in the early 1960s, there was concern from some quarters, but for others the project promised to strengthen the upward trend of progress and prosperity enjoyed by Campbell River citizens in postwar years, continuing the expansion of services, housing, retail opportunities and infrastructure precipitated by the influx of workers and families after Crown Zellerbach's Elk Falls pulp and paper mill opened in 1952.[6]

In the case of Strathcona, "the Class A status covering the park accepted prospecting and mining if claims were proved and developed within a two year period."[7] So Strathcona Park was open to some industry, and it compared to Class B parks that "were designated where conflicting resource tenures existed or where the Province was prepared to tolerate them, meaning they were open to multiple use."[8]

The Bedwell River area, long the site of mineral claims, was reclassified as "B" in the early 1960s, but the area at the southwestern end of Buttle Lake, where Western Mines had its original claims, remained under Class A status in the early part of the decade.[9] This, however, did not keep Western Mines from confidently buying twenty-three key claims, staking new claims in 1961, and subsequently drilling at Myra Falls, which revealed massive sulphides of zinc, copper, lead and silver ores.[10] Eventually, in 1965, three Nature Conservancies, closed to power boats and development of mineral claims, would be set aside within the Park, and Recreation Areas were designated. The latter proved to be one of the most controversial aspects of this amendment, for as the public was to discover, "Recreation Area" was rhetorical sleight of hand, and, similar to Class B, opened up such areas to prospecting and mine development. Both Strathcona Park and Kokanee Park lost their Class A status, and the entire parks were changed to Class B, since the scope of development exceeded the limitations of Class A status. Considered to be a "watershed moment" in the history of Strathcona Park, changes implemented under Kiernan were made without any consultation with the public, since the Minister of Recreation and Conservation had the power to issue permits on his own.[11] Kiernan contended that he was "not prepared to recognize any mineral claim that has not been recorded"; however, since claims *had* been recorded at Myra Falls, this area would be open for mining. In a perplexing footnote he added, "... although none of this land will cease to be park."[12]

TOP Roderick Haig-Brown (left) and Jim Boulding (centre) attending an Eco conference, 1970. IMAGE MCR88-24B7F72D COURTESY OF THE MUSEUM AT CAMPBELL RIVER ARCHIVES

BOTTOM Strathcona Lodge newly situated at the top of the hill. MYRNA BOULDING COLLECTION

In an effort to eliminate any possible confusion, Alec Merriman, the outspoken writer of the Outdoors column in the *Daily Colonist*, wrote that "Minister Kiernan downgraded one-third of the most accessible parts of the park to Class B status to allow industry to exploit the park."[13]

Bob Ahrens, who began his career with BC Parks in 1949 and retired in 1984, visited Myra Falls when the lake was still pristine; in 1953 before it was flooded; and then again in the late 1950s before the mine went in. "We went up to the base of the falls and we could see the pebbles in the bottom." When he heard that the mine was to go ahead, he was told "it's only a ten acre hole in the ground."[14]

Roderick Haig-Brown noted that "their first ideas were disarmingly simple. Certainly the mine would be in a park, but it would be just a little mine, just a little hole confined to a few acres that wouldn't bother anyone." Wondering why the government had not attempted to purchase the claims, he was astonished at the pace of development and how quickly the already degraded Buttle Lake area faced the threat of a mine along with a proposed townsite.[15]

Equally alarmed at the advent of the industrialization of Strathcona Park were its nearest neighbours, Jim and Myrna Boulding. The Bouldings had purchased a 160 acre property on the east side of Upper Campbell Lake from Myrna's father, Wallace Baikie, in 1959, acreage Baikie had received from the Power Commission in exchange for land he lost when the lake flooded. Baikie and his brothers purchased the beautiful cedar tourist lodge, which Myrna had admired as a child, from the Power Commission for $500, and before the lake flooded, placed logs under the building so that it would float. A year later it settled at the bottom of their new property, and they towed it up to the top of the hill near the roadside. The property was just nine kilometres west of Strathcona Park along the road to Buttle Lake, and the Bouldings were concerned about noise from industrial traffic going to and from the mine.[16]

The Bouldings were friends of Roderick Haig-Brown. Myrna Boulding recalls hearing him speak at their convocation from

TOP Myrna and Jim Boulding in front of the Lodge, 1963. MYRNA BOULDING COLLECTION

BOTTOM The gravel road leading to Strathcona Park, 1960. MYRNA BOULDING COLLECTION

OPPOSITE Map showing Strathcona Lodge and end of the road, 1960. MYRNA BOULDING COLLECTION

teachers' college in Nanaimo in 1955, coming away impressed with his conservationist views. When the Bouldings moved from Nanaimo to Campbell River in 1958 to take teaching positions, they soon became well acquainted with Roderick and his wife, Ann, who socialized with Myrna's parents. Myrna also taught the Haig-Brown children at the local high school.[17]

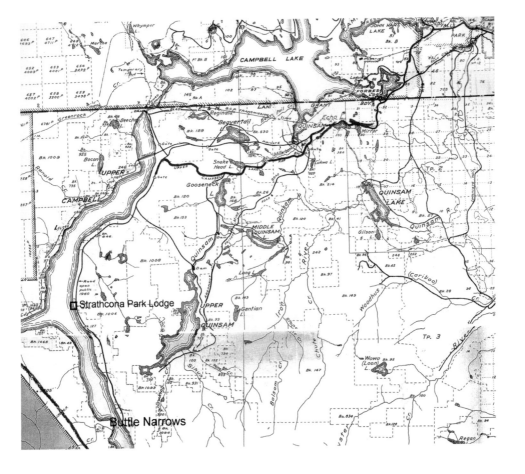

Just as Haig-Brown had advocated for improved road access to Buttle Lake ten years earlier, Jim Boulding and the Campbell River and District Chamber of Commerce in 1961 urged the government to improve the existing roads, citing increased tourist traffic, unaware that Western Mines would soon be instrumental in making the improvements they sought. The Bouldings' property sat on the gravel road that ran from Upper Campbell Lake to where it joined Buttle Lake at Buttle Narrows. This road was built by Baikie Bros. in 1958 on behalf of the Power Commission, after the first road they built was lost in valley flooding. The Chamber referred to this stretch of road as the "Million Dollar Road," complaining that it was connected to the original government road ending at Echo Lake (Camp 8) by nothing more than a "goat trail," a distance of

Men working at Western Mines' Myra Falls Operation, 1965. IMAGE MCR010734
COURTESY OF THE MUSEUM AT CAMPBELL RIVER ARCHIVES

about fifteen kilometres. The Chamber also requested construction of a trail along the east shore of Buttle Lake.[18]

Western Mines' intention to develop its claims at the south end of Buttle Lake in 1964 first involved construction of a road along the eastern shore of the lake so that crews and equipment would no longer have to go in and out by boat. When the perimeter of the lake was logged off in 1955 in preparation for flooding, crude logging roads would have been created. However, when Cattermole-Trethewey Contracting cleared the timber around the lake in 1956, they hauled all the timber out by water. Parks Department employees used the rough road to access the southern reaches of the lake, but it was not up to Western Mines' standards.

When Charlie Darkis, a Parks Department employee who worked out of the Miracle Beach regional office, was on a routine check of the south end of Buttle Lake in the early 1960s, he was startled to encounter men and equipment near Myra Falls and asked the crew what they were doing there. He told them they had to leave, but was promptly shown a permit for drilling. He had to concede that their permit looked legitimate and came from the highest source, Minister of Recreation and Conservation Kenneth Kiernan. While in conversation with the men, they complained to him that the road down to the falls was very winding and they weren't satisfied that it was useable for their purposes. Darkis didn't think he could do anything to help with that matter, but certainly felt he should report this meeting to his supervisors. He found upon his return that no one at Miracle Beach knew about the activities at Myra Falls, and even more surprising, neither did head office in Victoria.[19]

While the Parks Department over the years had been blamed for activities in the Park that were contrary to preservationist philosophy, this incident clearly illustrates the lack of power the Department had over decision making regarding Park use. Decisions were made at the top level of government, not only without consultation, but also without any warning.

Western Mines appealed to Kiernan for a new and improved road. In response, Kiernan agreed that a new public road would be built by the province's Department of Highways at a cost of $2 million, to be paid by the mining company.[20] "It is a sickening statement that access to parks is only possible through industrial development," Vancouver Island Wildlife Association president Ed Mankelow commented upon hearing this announcement.[21] The completed Western Mines road connected at Buttle Narrows with the new highway to Gold River, under construction in 1966. That project, linking the east coast of Vancouver Island to the west, coincided with the opening of the new Gold River pulp mill. By the late 1960s, the entire roadway from Campbell River to Buttle Narrows, the Western Mines road and the Gold River road were paved as a result of these developments, finally ending years of frustration for travellers on this route.[22]

For the Bouldings, the newly improved highway that ran in front of their property was a mixed blessing. While travellers could enjoy easier access to their resort, the increase in industrial traffic from a mine working on a twenty-four hour schedule meant the night time quiet the Bouldings, their guests and staff who lived on the property were accustomed to was disrupted by the rattle of ore trucks on the road in the early hours of the morning. Guests were known to complain and leave because of the traffic noise.[23] While this road and the one into Myra Falls offered better access to the park, it was difficult to accept that until a mining company decided to exploit the park's mineral riches, the province took no interest in local road building.

Newspapers offered conflicting views of how the public reacted to a mine in their once pristine park. For some it was another sign of the material prosperity that had spurred the Campbell River region's postwar growth, epitomized by the *Upper Islander*'s 1966 headline: "Western Mines Soon into Production: Old Claims in Strathcona Park Became Fabulous Success Story."[24] But the 1965 announcement that Western Mines intended to establish a town-site in the park disturbed all but the most ardent supporters. One local writer declared that Campbell River and the local Chamber of Commerce were "lead down the garden path as far as the real intentions of the company within the park was concerned."[25] A week after the announcement, Campbell River Fish and Game Club president George Bergsma informed club members they "would be gearing up for a long hard fight" against the entire proposed development, which was contrary to all concepts of park stewardship. "Parks are just too important to allow industrial development," he asserted. The president of the Campbell River branch of the BC Motels and Resorts Association, Harold McKeig, joined in and filed a protest against the development. In the end, the townsite would not be approved.[26]

Buttle Lake Pollution and Kiernan Kocktails

In the 1960s, an understanding of the ecological harm that a mine could wreak on a lake in a near-pristine environment was lacking, but it could not be denied that an open-pit mine would leave "a huge scar in an area that was set aside as a park because of its beauty."[27] Moreover, Western Mines had permission to dump tailings, the residue left after ore is separated from rock in the milling process, directly into the lake. A new controversy involving the park was to occupy the media and townspeople, who were afraid of what harm would come not only to fish, but also to their drinking water from tailings pollution.[28]

Just one month after the mine started operations in 1966, Jim Boulding and a few friends went to the mine site to investigate the state of Buttle Lake and were shocked to find a grey, sludge-like substance at the mouth of Myra Creek, originating from the tailings. In March 1967, Boulding was in Victoria along with at least one hundred Vancouver Island citizens staging a protest, waving placards denouncing the dumping of tailings into Buttle Lake, and as Myrna remembered, "dropped the goop on the stairs of the Legislature."[29]

Scientific research on the health of Buttle Lake and its fish population was conducted only intermittently throughout the early

1950s to mid-'60s. In 1953, fish biologist Peter Larkin conducted a biological survey of the lake for the British Columbia Game Commission prior to hydro-electric development, predicting that trout spawning areas would be lost if water levels rose. No further studies were conducted until the tailings issue arose, and one month after the Victoria protest, the Pollution Control Board met with Minister of Lands, Forests and Water Resources Ray Williston. They agreed to hire an independent expert, Dr. George Langford, to conduct a study.[30]

Remembered by Myrna Boulding as Longstaff, he stayed at the Lodge while undertaking his investigation:

> Longstaff, who was... supposedly an expert on such matters, came here to do a study. I am quite sure that this man never made it past our Lodge, but instead sat on our deck and drank a beverage of his choice. This so called expert then wrote a report saying that what the mine was doing was fine, that the thermocline would take care of the tailings, transferring them somehow to the bottom.[31]

Boulding may not have been convinced that Langford completed a thorough investigation; however, Langford submitted two reports and recommended establishing a research station at Buttle Lake so that water quality could be regularly monitored.[32] This was not carried out, and park defenders derisively referred to the foul smelling and cloudy lake waters at Myra Creek as "Kiernan Kocktails."[33] As a result of public pressure, in 1967, the mine built a settlement pond to capture tailings, but the runoff from this facility drained into Myra Creek and thence into Buttle Lake, the source of Campbell River's water supply.[34]

From 1971 to 1980, Western Mines, the Fish and Wildlife Branch and the Waste Management Department of the Ministry of Environment continued to test Buttle Lake's water for mineral content. Dr. Malcolm Clark with the Waste Management Department reported in 1980 that metal levels in the lake continued to be high,

TOP Sign upon entering Strathcona Park, 1970. MYRNA BOULDING COLLECTION

BOTTOM Jim Boulding (centre) with placard on steps of Legislature in Victoria. MYRNA BOULDING COLLECTION

and his findings were supported by the mining company's own consultant, Henry E. Jackson, who in that same year concluded that "tailings discharge alone could not explain the increased metal values in this lake, but that other major sources must also contribute to the metal loading."[35]

Clark was engaged once more to submit a report in 1982, precipitated by a proposal by the company, now known as Westmin Resources, to expand the mine and mill operation. At the time of his writing, the operations consisted of two inactive open-pit mines and three active underground mines—Lynx, Myra and Price—as well as a concentrator and one ore crushing plant. His study found that there was "a pattern of high metals content" in the vicinity of the operations and that "a serious deterioration of the water quality in the Buttle Lake–Campbell River watershed is emerging and is attributable... to the Westmin Resources Ltd. operations."[36]

The true extent and consequences of the presence of metals in the water did not become clear until a study was conducted that same year by Dr. Tom Pedersen, then with the Department of Oceanography at UBC. Pedersen was asked by Henry Jackson, who now chaired a panel assembled by the provincial government, to assess the effect of tailings going into Buttle Lake. Pedersen's first experience testing tailings was at the Island Copper mine in Rupert Inlet on north Vancouver Island in the 1970s, where high metals content in the ocean near the mine had been noted. There, much to his surprise, he found that rather than leaching minerals into the water, the tailings were actually absorbing them. While this seemed to hold true in salt water, his hypothesis was yet to be tested in fresh water.[37]

Testing the water in Buttle Lake for mineral content, he discovered levels of zinc approximately one hundred times the amount that would be considered a safe level for human consumption, along with high levels of copper, lead and cadmium. This was also clearly harmful to fish, as their numbers had declined dramatically since the mine began operations. As Clark noted in his 1982 report, zinc is "acutely toxic to salmonids." Even before Pedersen made his discoveries, earlier testing found that dissolved levels of copper and zinc along Myra Creek "do not meet water quality criteria."[38] But if the source of metals in the lake was not tailings, then what was it?

Pedersen explained in an interview that when the Myra Falls operation began digging the first open-pit mine, some bits of the ore below were scraped off along with soil, then stacked as a waste dump within the mine site. These bits and pieces of ore and pyrite, when exposed to oxygen and rain, went through a process of sulphide oxidizing. The resulting by-product was sulphuric acid. The acid then dissolved minerals in the rock present in the waste dump, leaching zinc, lead, copper and cadmium from the ores. This toxic mix washed into Myra Creek in massive amounts, explaining the extremely high concentrations of minerals where the creek meets the lake. There was no awareness of this process in the 1960s, when the mine went in, but with Pedersen's findings, Westmin was ordered to collect water from the waste dump and to dig a half-metre-deep ditch around the dump. The drainage is now collected and goes through a treatment plant, where lime dries up the hydroxides, effectively reducing most of the dissolved metal.

At the same time, in late 1982, Westmin also constructed tailings ponds away from Myra Creek, although Pedersen was never convinced that this solved the problem of Buttle Lake pollution and believes the ponds were built merely to pacify the public. Although Pedersen submitted his report to the province, he believed it was never released, and he did not talk about his findings. In retrospect, he felt he should have spoken up, since he now believes it is the role of a scientist to be a "watch dog."[39]

"DON'T CUT THE HEART OUT OF STRATHCONA PARK"

Possibly the shortest trip from the base of Buttle Lake near Shepherd Creek to put the visitor in touch with snow, ice, and fantastic mountains with marble cliffs, is to the head of Phillips Creek. Here mountain meadows, heather-fields, lakelets, and snow-clad marble peaks abound, their faces polished smooth as glass by driving snows, and marble-floored plateaus are strewn with great fragments in unutterable confusion. On this plateau are numbers of wells or blow-holes of unknown depth, filled with snow or ice in part, and doubtless further explorations will reveal caves.

STRATHCONA PARK, VANCOUVER ISLAND
pamphlet from the BC Department of Lands, 1921

DESPITE THE PRESENCE of a mine in Strathcona Park, the park figured largely in future plans for Strathcona Park Lodge. A trip to England in 1969 convinced Jim and Myrna Boulding that their business should be catering to those interested in a comprehensive outdoor experience. Visiting Outward Bound Centres, where the focus was on teaching outdoor skills such as mountain climbing and rock climbing, they envisioned transforming their property into an outdoor education centre. The Lodge's proximity to Strathcona Park presented exceptional opportunities for hiking, camping and mountain climbing, and its location on Upper Campbell Lake made it ideal for water sports such as kayaking and canoeing. Coupled with their increasing interest in environmental stewardship through their friend Haig-Brown, and their experience as teachers, they developed a philosophy that incorporated ideals of self-reliance, survival, fitness, health, outdoor skills and respect for the environment, including leave no trace hiking and camping. Due to a paucity of outdoor education instructors in Canada, the first instructors came from Britain, followed by several American draft dodgers and counterculture youth attracted to the outdoors and "back to the earth" lifestyle practised at the Lodge.[1]

By the early 1970s, the Bouldings' centre offered instruction to high school and elementary teachers and accepted groups of school children for week-long outdoor courses, while continuing to welcome tourists.[2] Office staff provided information about

TOP Strathcona Lodge mountaineering students practising crevasse rescue in Strathcona Park. MYRNA BOULDING COLLECTION

BOTTOM Rob and Laurie Wood celebrating their wedding at Strathcona Lodge, early 1970s. MYRNA BOULDING COLLECTION

Strathcona Park to guests, as well as to passing motorists. By the end of the '70s, the Bouldings had developed the Apprenticeship Program, involving British mountaineers such as Jim Rutter, Steve Smith and Rob Wood, to train outdoor recreation leaders in Canada. The relative remoteness of the Lodge meant that staff lived on the property, and in peak season upward of seventy-five people would make up this small community. In this intimate setting, where staff ate, slept and socialized together, close relationships developed quickly, and the Bouldings, fully immersed in the everyday running of their business, became friends and mentors to many.

Jim Boulding stands out as an advocate for tourism and ecological interests, although opinions of his depth of commitment differ. Rob Wood reminisced that "Jim Boulding was a man from whom I learned more than anyone else and a man whose teaching has influenced a whole generation of British Columbians and outdoors people from all over the world."[3] Wood learned from Boulding such concepts as "stewardship of the land," emphasizing that all human beings were responsible for overseeing and protecting the natural world. Boulding was extremely outspoken and determined; one writer observed that he was "a big man who doesn't believe in rolling over for anyone," including park managers who he criticized for a "lack of consideration in their stewardship of Strathcona."[4] Some friends of Boulding's, however, did not view him as a true environmentalist, since "he was concerned about the environment when it suited him," and cited his affection for motorized boats and heavy duty trucks, and his unabashed use of helicopters to take skiers into the park.[5]

For her part, Myrna Boulding expressed her opinions in well-penned letters to any officials who she thought were misinformed or needed to be informed about actual events. In 1983, a new difficulty with the Parks and Outdoor Recreation Division of the Ministry of Lands, Parks and Housing took the Bouldings by surprise. Shortly after Jim raised the alarm about a fire in Strathcona Park at Auger Point and assisted with fighting the fire, he and Myrna received a letter from Ken Baker, the manager, Operations

Section, at Parks, informing them that they would have to start paying for permits to take their clients into the park. In an August 30 letter directed to Baker, Myrna wrote:

Dear Sirs:

I have been going to rewrite my original answer to your letter of June 4 all summer but have not been able to figure out what to say. I have decided to send my original reply.

In respect to your request that we require a park use permit for our trips, I would like to enter into some sort of a dialogue with you or someone in your department.

1. As you may be aware we have been using the park for twenty-three years with no mention of a permit required.

2. Over the last twelve or so years we have dealt with approximately 5,000 school and university students per year teaching them outdoor education.

3. Two of the things we stress with all of our guests are wilderness ethics and low impact camping.

4. Our adventure holiday trips have grown out of teaching education courses that we used to run.

5. We are not a business in the usual sense. As you can see by the enclosed list our education programmes are backed by a foundation.

6. We particularly stress the use of quiet boats i.e. Canoes, kayaks, sail boats, windsurfers.

7. We promote the use of helicopters only for people who are unable to walk the considerable distance into the alpine in Strathcona Park, and then not into the Nature Conservancy areas (we were only told this rule last year).

8. We feel we are good neighbours to the park and do more than almost any other group to teach and promote good attitudes and

the right use of the wilderness. We also have put out at least 6 fires in the park since we came here.

9. At the same time we are vastly unhappy about some other users of the park:

   a) Western Mines—need I say more (the trout fishing is terrible— the water polluted)

   b) A gold prospector madly staking the whole area for a foreign company—he seems somewhat eccentric and carried two powerful revolvers in holsters. He claims to have found a boulder with $20,000 worth of gold in this area.

   c) Recently the industrial traffic past our place, particularly ore trucks from Western Mines has been truly frightening.

10. We expect that this sudden interest in us is a result of my husband being interviewed on National T.V. about park policy in respect to fire watch, and the use of water bombers. Unfortunately, this debate deteriorated into an irrelevant argument about who phoned in the first (the telephone company said that we did). His information about the water bomber policy was from a good government source.

11. We are also unhappy that the Parks Branch couldn't give us any of the fire damaged wood last winter although they gave it to the cadets and also, according to a driver we talked to, to the air force.

    You must understand that we really care about this park and are more concerned about its long term survival than are, it appears, some civil servants and politicians. We have spent years trying to beautify the area at the entrance to the park, by removing stumps, removing debris from the lake, bringing in soil and sand, planting trees etc; in other words trying to repair the damage done by hydro development on this watershed.

    You should read the diaries in the archives written by the early surveyors, people with profound vision. They would be horrified by what has happened to their beautiful park.

We do not want to fight with the Parks Branch. It seems during these troubled times that co-operation might mean survival for both of us. I just had a British guest leave this morning because the lorries kept her awake. The industrial traffic to Western Mines is steady from three a.m. on. I also hear the forestry has given approval for Elk Mountain to be logged. This is the beautiful mountain at the entrance to the park shown in the large picture (reversed) in our brochure. The ensuing mess and debris will probably mean our Waterloo.

Yours truly,

Myrna Boulding
Owner/Manager[6]

Jim Boulding's concern for the park, despite his other less than ecological actions, was genuine, and in 1985, there were developments in park policy that alarmed him and other recreational users of the park. For more than a decade, Strathcona Park had enjoyed protection from further resource extraction. The New Democratic Party (NDP) had come into power in 1972, and a year later placed a moratorium on mining in parks that essentially changed Class B areas to Class A, protecting these areas from development.[7] The government also had plans to conduct a study into existing mineral claims, which numbered about 400, to see if it was feasible to purchase them. In this atmosphere of positive change, as well, in June 1974, Parks director Bob Ahrens announced there was a proposal to alter the boundaries of the Park so that they would conform with contours of land and the location of watersheds. Buttle Lake, for example, would be wholly situated within the Park rather than be only two thirds within it.[8] None of these initiatives were followed through at that time, possibly because the NDP was only in power for three years.

The Social Credit Party (Socreds) returned to power in 1975, and there were no proposed changes in Strathcona Park until 1985 when, confronted by widespread park land use conflicts, the

STRATHCONA PROVINCIAL PARK

BOUNDARIES and CLASSIFICATION

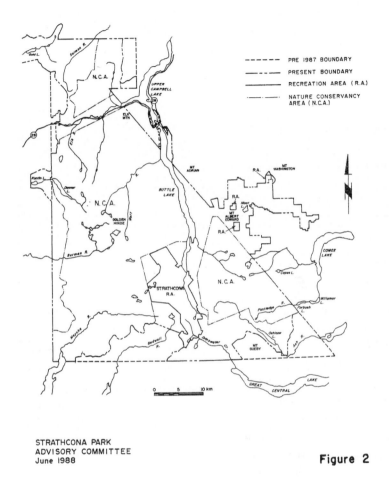

STRATHCONA PARK
ADVISORY COMMITTEE
June 1988

Figure 2

Map of Boundary Classifications, 1986. FROM THE REPORT OF THE STRATHCONA
PARK ADVISORY COMMITTEE, JIM RUTTER COLLECTION

government formed the Wilderness Advisory Committee (WAC).
The WAC report, the *Wilderness Mosaic*, advised deletions and
additions to Strathcona Park, as well as classification changes

Marlene (at left) and Steve Smith (right) at Strathcona Lodge, early 1970s.

that would facilitate another mining operation near the Westmin Resources site where Cream Silver Mines Ltd. had claims, stating specifically that the "mineralized belt, including the Westmin Mine and Cream Lake, should be designated a Recreation Area."[9]

Correctly interpreting that designation as a licence to mine, activists would form the Friends of Strathcona Park (FOSP) and mount a major protest against boundary changes and exploratory drilling in the park. This led to the creation of the Strathcona Advisory Committee in March 1988 to gather public input, which in turn gave rise to the 1993 Master Plan for Strathcona Park.

When Jim Boulding attended the "Wilderness Mosaic" meeting in Campbell River presented by the WAC in 1985, Marlene Smith, a Strathcona Lodge outdoor instructor, remembered how shocked he was to hear of the proposal to cut out large sections of the park or alter park status to facilitate logging or mining claims and explorations. Boulding told the Committee in no uncertain terms that one could not sell "second hand wilderness."[10]

Boulding was ill with pancreatic cancer at this time, and Rob Wood observed that the negative news seemed to worsen his condition. As Wood witnessed Boulding struggling with his illness, he pledged to carry on with the fight to preserve Strathcona's wilderness values. He wrote:

> My good friends, Stevey and Marlene Smith, had known Jim at his best and were deeply affected, both by his generosity of spirit and his love of Nature—Strathcona Park in particular. They knew that his love was their love and they also decided to take Jim's stewardship baton and run with it.[11]

Jim had in fact asked Marlene Smith to "take over the torch" from him and his "old friend Roderick Haig-Brown."[12] She took this request to heart and has done so fiercely ever since.

For Steve, who was from England, and Marlene, from Holland, Strathcona Park was astonishing. The sight of this huge area of pristine wilderness, where there were few trails and no power poles, was something that did not exist in Europe. "We were breathless," she acknowledged.[13]

Not knowing where to begin, on Myrna Boulding's suggestion Smith wrote to former Lodge staff member Susanne Lawson in Tofino, asking for guidance and assistance with formulating a strategy to thwart the Socred government's apparent plan to permit further mining activity in the park. Lawson and her husband, Steven, had been successful in saving old growth trees on Meares Island, near their home in Tofino, from being logged, and they were part of a growing contingent of wilderness protectors in British Columbia, such as the Western Canada Wilderness Committee, the Valhalla Wilderness Society, Canadian Parks and Wilderness Society, and Friends of Ecological Reserves.[14] As hikers, mountaineers and guides for Strathcona Lodge, Marlene and Steve Smith had come to know Strathcona Park well and enjoyed passing on their passion for preserving nature to the children they taught. As Marlene told Susanne Lawson,

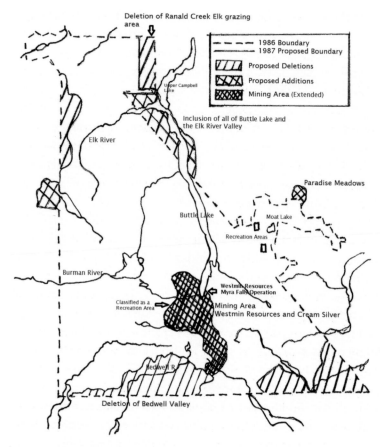

Map of Strathcona Provinical Park showing 1987 Proposed Deletions and Additions

Total Park Area in 1986: 231,000 hectares
Proposed Deletions: 36,000 hectares
Proposed Additions: 6,000 hectares

Map of proposed additions and deletions, 1986 and 1987. ADAPTED FROM
1986/87 BEFORE AND AFTER MAPS, SUSANNE LAWSON COLLECTION

We were therefore very concerned after reading the proposals
of the [Wilderness Advisory] committee—especially to delete
35000 hectares of the Park and to change the Tennant Lake–
Cream Lake area to a "Recreation Area" status. We understand
this would allow mining expansion. We are aware that the area

is possibly rich in minerals and that an extension to the already existing "eye-sore" of Westmin Mines at the south end of this beautiful Buttle Lake would no doubt create a few more jobs.[15]

She went on to explain that she had already been in touch with several concerned groups such as the Valhalla Wilderness Society, formed in 1975, which had been successful in turning a potential logging site into a park.[16] Now she was hoping to formulate a plan. How did these groups of activists get organized? What drove them? A first meeting, hosted by the BC Federation of Mountain Clubs, was to be held April 5, 1986, in Nanaimo. The Lawsons joined forces with the Smiths, and each from their respective coasts of Vancouver Island worked toward the goal of safeguarding Strathcona Park against further degradation.

Jim Boulding passed away in May 1986 at the age of fifty-two, just before he was to receive the Heaslip Award for Environmental Stewardship, and that summer the Smiths, Rob Wood and another friend, Noel Lax, came up with the idea of forming the Friends of Strathcona Park (FOSP) as a means of galvanizing support for their concerns.[17] The Friends established their headquarters in Parksville and set up local chapters in other communities in the vicinity of Strathcona Park. Amidst growing concerns about stewardship of the Park, BC Parks officials led celebrations for the 75th anniversary of the founding of Strathcona Park.[18]

For Smith, the process of lobbying for the right to be heard was an eye-opener about politics, and she felt that leaders and ministers "didn't have a clue."[19] Her inherent commitment to fight for what she thought was right kept her motivated. She felt that she had probably, in many ways, inherited this determination from her parents, who resisted German occupation of Holland during the Second World War. She learned at a young age that nothing is written in stone. "If you believe, you just do it."

Minister of Environment Stephen Rogers had promised public hearings to discuss deletions from the park in 1986, but they did not materialize, and in January 1987 he announced his intention to "implement the recommendations of the Wilderness Advisory Committee to allow for more mining in parks."[20] When it was revealed that Rogers had financial interests in Westmin, he was dismissed in March over the conflict of interest, and replaced by Bruce Strachan.[21]

Once they received word of this announcement, the Friends approached nearby municipalities, voicing their concerns, and in the spring of 1987 were successful in garnering letters of support from the Regional District of Campbell River, the City of Parksville, Town of Qualicum Beach and the Regional District of Comox-Strathcona that were directed to both Premier Bill Vander Zalm and Bruce Strachan, requesting public hearings before boundary and classification changes in the park could take effect.[22] Membership in the Friends was growing, and they were attracting well-known advocates for wilderness protection such as journalist Des Kennedy, who would later take a hand in organizing demonstrations in Strathcona Park, and the Comox Valley's Ruth Masters. By 1987, membership had risen to 150, with numbers swelling to 1,400 the following year.[23]

On May 7, Susanne Lawson, as head of the Lawsons' business, Ecological Management Enterprises, wrote to Bruce Strachan, reiterating that all communities near Strathcona Park desired input into decisions made about the park. Questioning the Ministry of Environment's competence to make informed recommendations, and attacking the government's multiple use philosophy, she went on to declare that "logging, mining and tourism don't mix." Lawson advised Strachan that the FOSP believed the Ministry should initiate a Royal Commission to study the park areas slated for exclusion and alteration.[24]

In an effort to justify the Ministry of Environment's open-for-business strategy for park policy, Strachan's department produced a publication in January 1988 entitled *Striking the Balance*. The issue of shifting park boundaries was adroitly handled by the statement that, "Over time, our park system has developed with boundary adjustments and a flexibility to social requirements. During periods when stimulating the economy was paramount, parks have been opened to resource extraction."[25]

Just six months later, the report based on public input, *Restoring the Balance*, authored by the Strachan-appointed Strathcona Advisory Committee, identified that it was this very strategy that was at the heart of controversy surrounding Strathcona Park. "It is a widespread perception," the authors state, "that the Parks Division is perennially giving up pieces of Strathcona Park to the benefit of industry."[26]

When Cream Silver Mines Ltd. began drilling its claims in Strathcona Park in 1988, it seemed the worst fears of the park's would-be protectors had come true.

Cream Silver's interest in developing its claims dated back to 1967. At that time it had secured permission to extend the Buttle Lake Road to its site, eight kilometres south of the existing Myra Falls mine. Cream Silver president Frank Lang, aware of public concern over Western Mines beginning operations the year before, said he expected "none of the controversy that erupted with development of Western Mines."[27] However, when Western Mines' pollution of Buttle Lake became an issue and precipitated further studies, Cream Silver's exploration was put on hold.[28]

The NDP's 1973 moratorium on mining development in the park further delayed Cream Silver's exploration plans, but in 1987, when the Socreds gave the area of Cream Silver's claims Recreation Area status, the company applied for an exploration permit. This time, when Cream Silver announced its intention to begin drilling in January of 1988, Buttle Lake pollution appeared to be a non-issue.[29]

Karl Stevenson, an FOSP member hiking in Strathcona Park that same month, alerted Steve and Marlene Smith to Cream Silver's drilling activities, and he asked for their help in blockading the mining company's access to the site. Although not all FOSP members were in favour of participating in the blockade, eventually hundreds of people made their way to the drilling site, camping in the dead of winter and carrying on a peaceful protest, waving placards with the FOSP slogan: "Don't Cut the Heart Out of Strathcona Park."[30]

Teresa Strukoff, who was residing at Strathcona Lodge that winter, was among a contingent of other Lodge residents who joined in. They and a number of protesters who were staying as guests at the Lodge reached the remote spot in a bus supplied by the Lodge, even though, officially, the Lodge did not want to appear to be directly supporting them. Nonetheless, Myrna Boulding contacted her friend, well-known environmental activist David Suzuki, to alert him to the action. He came and spoke at a large rally held in January at the Ralph River at the south end of the park, lending his star power to the proceedings.[31]

Other high profile activists such as David (Walrus) Garrick and Paul Watson, who had made a name for themselves during the formative years of Greenpeace in the mid-1970s, joined in to support the FOSP cause, taking upon themselves the task of laying rocks in the culverts alongside the road, thinking this might flood the road to the drilling site and make it impassable.[32]

First Nations leaders from the Nuu-Chah-Nulth Tribal Council, such as Archie Frank, and Wedlidi Speck of the Kwagiulth District Council met after the rally and agreed to support the FOSP against mining development in the Park. "The parks," said Speck, "are the closest thing to what we had before contact. We must preserve them—and that's true for us whether we're red, white, yellow or black."[33]

Strukoff recalled that although protesters were blocking the road and sometimes lying on top of machinery, they had all been attending workshops about conflict resolution and adhering to non-violent protest rules, such as "don't touch, fall down on the ground." In fact, they were asked to sign an agreement that specified it was important not to be obnoxious to police or those in authority. At these workshops, protesters were also instructed in how it felt to get arrested and warned that they might end up with a criminal record. What may have seemed like chaos at the time was, in fact, well organized. Strukoff was impressed with the number of participants who came from Tofino, the Comox Valley, and island communities such as Denman and Cortes to this isolated spot to show their solidarity. Initially skeptical about the protesters' capacity to make a difference, in the end she was astonished to realize that they were capable of changing a policy.[34]

Not all Lodge staff were willing to jump wholeheartedly into the fray. The Lodge's program director Karen Schwalm, who felt strongly that the Lodge should challenge Cream Silver, worried about the professional risks of direct involvement and decided not to "go against the law." Responsible for school and outdoor programs, Schwalm wanted to maintain a good rapport with school boards, and having collaborated on research projects with BC Parks, she was reluctant to jeopardize that relationship. She did, however, visit the protest site but refrained from such activities as climbing on machinery that might lead to her arrest. She was supportive of the Friends, remembering proudly, "I bought my T shirt." She thought that Myrna Boulding, responsible for the Lodge's image, shared her caution, but believes Jim would not have hesitated to get into the thick of it.

Both Schwalm and Strukoff recalled that when the Royal Canadian Mounted Police arrived to arrest protesters, they asked for volunteers since the jails did not have the capacity to hold everyone present.[35] The blockade lasted a total of two months, ending in March, and there were sixty-four arrests, although in the end, no one was charged.[36]

Cream Silver, in the meantime, did its best to mitigate the uproar. A meeting held in Campbell River saw the company's president, Frank Lang, express "sympathy" for the public's concerns about possible further environmental damage from mining. One disgusted observer left the meeting early, calling it a "love-in," and Comox-Strathcona Regional District Chairman Keith Hudson commented that mining in parks was "unreasonable." Several attendees agreed that there was little point in setting areas aside as parks only to permit logging and mining in them.[37]

One month later, the mining company took out a full page advertorial in the *Campbell River Mirror* that proposed to educate the public about the mining process. Lang explained that "we are taking this opportunity to provide you with some factual information about our activities," assuring readers that they were properly permitted and the drilling site was not pristine, the forest there having burned. He reiterated that his company was aware of environmental concerns, and further expressed hope that the recently established Special Advisory Committee "will resolve the policy issues involved."[38]

The Ministry of the Environment's 1988 Spring issue of *Strathcona Park News* introduced the Strathcona Advisory Committee (SAC), headed up by fisheries biologist Dr. Peter Larkin, then vice-president of research at the University of British Columbia. Larkin had also served on the Wilderness Advisory Committee (WAC) which had come so heavily under fire over the boundary changes it recommended for Strathcona Park. Other members of the SAC were Windsor Plywood owner Frances Jones of Qualicum Beach, lawyer Roderick Naknakim of the Quadra Island Cape Mudge Band, and Jim Rutter of Victoria, who came from a five-year term as the executive director of the Federation of Mountain Clubs of BC (FMCBC).[39] Rutter had also been an outdoor education instructor at Strathcona Park Lodge in the late 1970s, working and living with Rob Wood and Steve Smith. In those years, he came to know the park well as he climbed its mountains and led groups on expeditions.[40]

While he was with the FMCBC, Rutter participated in the organization's role of identifying wilderness areas and working with the Ministry of Forests and BC Parks to help officials recognize parks as more than just "lines on maps." This background assisted him with his role on the SAC, working toward solutions to the concerns raised by the public. "The clamour from the FOSP, blockades and the press was so strong," he said, "that the government had to be seen to be doing something about it."[41]

Rutter recalled the process as "brutal" and one that came at the cost of friendship. The SAC held ten public hearings throughout Vancouver Island between mid-May and mid-June, then was tasked with writing a report. During the process, Rutter came to appreciate Peter Larkin's abilities as "an excellent listener." At the public hearing in Campbell River, Rutter was disappointed that Steve Smith, a former friend, called him a "sell out" for working with the "enemy," the government. Rutter believed he was invited to participate on the SAC because he supported "maximizing the wilderness conservation designation of Strathcona Park," and was "willing to work on the process, and not just be angry."[42]

The Committee reviewed 224 submissions before proceeding with its report.[43] A key submission from the Friends, written by their president, Dr. Bruce Wood, makes particular mention of the issue of acid mine waste pollution, referring to a 1985 Ministry of the Environment report. Wood asked how the establishment of another "acid generating mine" in the Campbell River Municipality's watershed could even be considered.[44]

The SAC issued its report in September of 1988, coinciding with Strachan's replacement as Environment Minister by Terry Huberts.[45] When FOSP founding member Noel Lax read it, he had "tears in his eyes," believing that the recommendations were just right.[46]

The report recommended creation of a Steering Committee to write a Master Plan for Strathcona Park,[47] and in 1989, Deputy Minister of Parks Jake Maselink invited Rutter, Peggy Carswell of Courtenay and Gold River mayor Ann Fiddick, as well as three Parks Division members, including Ron Quilter and Ron Lampard, to participate.[48] Marlene Smith was pleased to see Maselink's involvement, feeling that he "had a heart for the Park." To her mind, he acted according to the law and had integrity. He was not willing to see the Park given up to industry.[49]

Ann Fiddick, aware that there was tremendous concern about how the park was being "fractured," believed she was asked to be on the Committee because she represented the west side of the island. The Steering Committee's members came to their task with personal links and some shared commitments, although they also had their differences. During her tenure as mayor of Gold River, Fiddick effectively lobbied to have the Gold and Donner Lakes included in the park. She also served as a board member of the Comox-Strathcona District, where she first met fellow board member Peggy Carswell. She had never met Jim Rutter, but the two shared a connection with Myrna and the late Jim Boulding. Fiddick knew the Bouldings as she often stopped at the Lodge, the halfway point on Highway 28 on her treks back and forth to Gold River.[50]

"Struggling through that Master Plan was painful," Fiddick recalls. The Cream Silver mine issue was just the "tip of the iceberg"—BC Hydro, timber tenures and other mineral claims all needed consideration. The task required listening to a multitude of demands from the public. "Everything exploded like fireworks—this and that group all had issues that were all a little different." Fiddick knew Marlene Smith as the veterinarian for her horses and was aware of the FOSP's demands, such as prohibiting helicopters and float planes from entering the park. Feeling this was unreasonable, she would strive to find a middle ground.[51]

She considered that fellow committee member Peggy Carswell was not only sympathetic to the Friends but was "in sync with the 'Comox Valley Crazies,'" represented by such "rabid environmentalists" as Carswell's boyfriend, FOSP member Kel Kelly. However, Fiddick believed that protesters had to be radical to get the process started, even if that meant lying down in front of Cream Silver's machines. She herself had visited the blockade site and shared soup with the protesters. She had great respect for Ruth Masters and the other "old gals" who lived by their convictions. She saw Jim Rutter's contribution as valuable since he brought the perspective of an outdoor enthusiast who knew the park intimately, as Fiddick did, epitomized by such knowledge as "where the elk were." Above all, in her role as mayor of Gold River, she was compelled to do a practical job for her community so that it was properly represented in the finalized Plan.[52]

Three drafts of the Plan were eventually released in 1992 and simply labelled X, Y and Z. Much to the Friends' delight, all three versions leaned toward reclassifying the park to Class A status and disallowing further mining or logging. Their preference was for version "X," which maximized wilderness values for the park.[53] As Wood explains, "The Government would expand the park beyond its old boundaries, settle the mining and logging claims and consolidate the preservation of the Park in a statute law."[54] There would be no new mines in the park, although Westmin's Myra Falls mining operation would remain active.

Keeping its promise, the government purchased all outstanding mining claims in 1990, including Walter Guppy's. For Guppy, the "lucky strike" that he had been chasing all his adult life came from a wholly unexpected quarter; he confessed in an interview that he had eked out a meagre living as a miner, but, he said, the payout from the government buying out his claims "set me up for life... it was a big break for me."[55]

In 1993 the formal Master Plan was published, acknowledging that the process of creating a master plan for Strathcona Park, begun in 1987, had to be put on hold "principally in response to strong criticism about the government's intention to delete 30,431 hectares (approximately 65,000 acres) from the park without a recommended process of public hearings." The Ministry's new promise under the Master Plan was to "work with government agencies, regional districts, the public, industry and private land holders to protect wildlife, recreation and aesthetic values along park boundaries and control access into wilderness areas."[56] The issue that had precipitated the formation of the FOSP in 1986 regarding park boundaries was finally resolved.

CREATION OF A MASTER PLAN AND CONTEMPORARY HISTORY TO 2020

About 1,000 feet south from here is Lady Falls,
new beauties appearing in them with every trip.
The walls of the canyon near the falls are draped
with rare ferns, and the colours of many flowers
are seen through the mists like short sections of
the rainbows which during certain hours of the
day ornament the spray. It is told that a somewhat
cold-blooded individual climbed to the summit of
this ridge thinking to gaze on the reported views
with scorn, but on his arrival forgot his companions
and all else, and, until interrupted, gazed at the
views, repeating, as if entranced, "Wonderful;
wonderful; wonderful."

STRATHCONA PARK, VANCOUVER ISLAND
pamphlet from the BC Department of Lands, 1921

THE YEAR 1993 marked a new beginning in the history of Strathcona Provincial Park. The Master Plan spelled out in clear language the Ministry of Environment, Lands and Parks' objectives, acknowledging that input from several agencies, as well as the public, would be used in decision making. Most importantly, it was recommended that in order to implement the goals and objectives of the Master Plan, a Strathcona Park Public Advisory Committee (SPPAC), composed of members of the public, should be formed.[1]

Philip Stone has served as Chair of the SPPAC for numerous years, and in *Exploring Strathcona Park* he explains that the role of the Committee is purely advisory. Voting on management planning is not part of the proceedings, and meetings are attended by representatives of BC Parks such as Andy Smith, Area Supervisor at Miracle Beach. There are eleven public members from various backgrounds, such as geologist Hardolph Wasteneys, whose role was as liaison with the mine at Myra Falls, but who now is the SPPAC chairman.[2] The mine is currently owned by Nyrstar, and after a hiatus of about three years beginning in 2015, the company has recommenced operations.[3]

Ann Fiddick served on the Committee for several years and advocated for more rangers in the Park.[4] Although thirty new positions were created throughout BC Parks in 2017, Strathcona remained with Andy Smith as the only full-time ranger in his role as Area Supervisor, one senior ranger and one seasonally employed backcountry ranger.[5]

Fiddick was also on the Committee in 2007 when a new issue arose concerning horse use in parks. John and Adele Caton, managers of Clayoquot Wilderness Resort (CWR) on the west coast of Vancouver Island, submitted a proposal to BC Parks to upgrade the old road corridor to make a trail from Bedwell Sound up to the Bedwell Lakes, with the intention that resort guests could access the lower portion of the road on horseback. The Master Plan states: "On a trial basis, two areas have been designated for horse riding and other areas will be reviewed. These locations have minimal conflict with other users and can withstand this type of use." This was interpreted to mean that horses could be allowed in the Bedwell Valley portion of the Park.[6]

The issue reveals that Strathcona Park's use remains contentious today, even among those who have defended its integrity as they grapple with issues far more subtle than mining. The FOSP immediately objected to horse use, since this was not in line with their notion of the Park as a pristine environment, and there was a history of horseback riders leaving a mess in Forbidden Plateau. Not only did horse hooves destroy plant life and wear down trails on the Plateau, but horses would graze in and damage the meadows. Ruth Masters waded into the debate, concerned that allowing horse use "could set a precedent for other park plunderers."[7]

Myrna Boulding, on the other hand, supported the idea, writing that

> the Bedwell Trail in question is at present poorly maintained and used by very few people. In exchange for being able to take horses along the old road bed, the Catons have promised to make it possible for more than just the super fit to access this beautiful area. This will involve a lot of time and money to be spent on a continuing basis.[8]

Myrna's partner Brian Gunn, then president of the Wilderness Tourism Association of BC, also sided with the Catons, along with Ann Fiddick. This caused a temporary rift between these supporters of the Catons and Marlene Smith. Aware that all three were horse lovers, she felt they did not have the best interests of the Park at heart on this issue.

Since the old road bed had been washed out, the CWR recognized the need to build either new pedestrian bridges or formal fords. Guests would be guided along the gravel road bed up to Ashwood Creek (originally You Creek) to an elevation of about 100 metres. There was not a proposal to take riders into the sensitive alpine.

Interestingly, Andy Smith notes: "The Master Plan had identified a couple of locations that allowed potential horse use, but the question remained as to why this was the case. We learned that no studies/research had ever been done on horse use and therefore no real criteria set other than the use of road corridors." He went on to say that not only did the Bedwell area fit the criteria for horse use, but Wilderness Recreation zoning does allow horse use.[9]

A decision note was prepared for the Environment Minister, Barry Penner, who felt that research should be done, with impact assessments and criteria developed for horse use, followed by assessing all of Strathcona Park against the new criteria to determine where horse use should be allowed. "This," Smith said," would ensure that we have the tools we need to make decisions in the future."[10]

When the research was completed, an amendment was made to the Master Plan in 2010 that specifically related to horse use in the Park. CWR's permit application was assessed and approved according to the new criteria, albeit with strict conditions.

The FOSP had several reasons for feeling uncomfortable with the decision made by Parks, aside from historical damage of Forbidden Plateau. Marlene Smith felt that from her perspective as a veterinarian the Bedwell trail was simply not safe for horses: horseshoes had been found in the Bedwell River, signifying that horses had possibly thrown their shoes along the way. In her opinion, the Park as a whole was not horse terrain, as there was a danger of horse manure introducing invasive species, and conversely, horses would be prone to predation by cougars. The trail was washed out and was too steep for safe riding. She didn't believe that CWR was going to improve it. She was also concerned that while CWR promised to build sleeping platforms for its guests, these platforms would not necessarily be open to the public, especially at times when CWR guests were there.[11]

The Catons were prepared to address these concerns. While some areas of the Park were certainly not horse terrain, road beds could be, especially once improvements were made. Andy Smith explained that the road bed in question was not too steep for horses, as the horses would not be climbing up into the alpine—in fact, they were traversing a rather flat area up to a turnaround that ended at Ashwood Creek. With respect to manure, the wranglers planned to collect it, and all horses used in the Park would be quarantined and fed sterilized feed. It was also felt that danger from cougars was no greater within the Park than outside it. There appeared to be a misunderstanding regarding access to sleeping platforms, as they had to be open for the public as part of the permit conditions. According to Andy Smith, the CWR planned to make improvements for the good of the Park and for public use, not just the use of its guests.[12]

When the FOSP was working on the trail above the road bed from Bedwell Lake to Ashwood Creek in 1998, they found it difficult to work with the resort. When they heard that the decision was made in the resort's favour, the FOSP perceived that the Master Plan had been changed to accommodate the resort, when in fact the Master Plan was amended to create clarity and consistency in regards to horse use in the entire Park.[13] Nonetheless, they reasoned that if horses were allowed on the lower Bedwell road bed, riders could in fact access the alpine past Ashwood Creek if they wished to do so.[14]

In 2012, the FOSP petitioned the court to overturn the minister's decision. BC Parks was perceived to be selling out to private interests, and the only benefit would be to high-end resort clients. "Compromise," said Marlene Smith, "is not part of my dictionary."[15]

According to Andy Smith, Minister Penner believed that the "decision was made after careful consideration of relevant factors and the decision to issue the PUP [Park Use Permit] is subject to judicial review on a reasonableness standard, not a correctness standard... [and] the decision was reasonable."[16]

While the FOSP were disappointed with the decision, Marlene said she would listen to what the river had to say. "A voice in my head told me, the river has always taken care of itself."[17]

In the end, although the resort had received permission to go ahead with its plans, new owners took over in 2014, the Catons left their management positions and the plans never materialized.[18]

The Formation of the Strathcona Wilderness Institute

Marlene Smith writes today that "We can never let our vigilance down."[19] The FOSP that she helped form has a much smaller membership than it did in the days when so many came on board to protest against the Cream Silver mine, but the core membership remains active, maintaining a website and producing a newsletter. Smith's husband, Steve, along with Betty Brooks and other former 1980s activists such as Peggy Carswell, was instrumental in creating a new organization with the initial help of the FOSP, the Strathcona Wilderness Institute (SWI).[20] Incorporated in 1995, the SWI operates in the Comox Valley as a non-profit organization dedicated to protecting the Park for recreational users, teaching wilderness ethics and improving facilities for Park visitors, working alongside BC Parks to help fill gaps in the agency's services. Betty Brooks helped train park interpreters of natural history hired by the Strathcona Wilderness Institute after BC Parks cut its interpretation programs in 2002.[21]

Andy Smith has confirmed that BC Parks continues to be a firm supporter of the SWI, which operates both an information centre at Paradise Meadows that offers maps, souvenirs and hikes, and an occasional information hut at Buttle Lake, and explained that BC Parks has always tried to secure annual funding to help support it. This funding has taken different forms, and over the years, the amount has also varied. This became especially important in 2002, when a new provincial government slashed the budget of the already underfunded Parks department. Smith, who had joined BC Parks as an Extension Officer responsible for interpretive programs, taking over from Bill Merilees, as well as signage, communications, community engagement, partnerships and standards, found his position eliminated. "This decision," he said, "severely restricted BC Parks communication and interaction with the public."[22]

He also explained that replacing and maintaining aging facilities was severely restricted due to lack of funding, which resulted in some facilities temporarily closing. In his new position as Area Supervisor specifically for Strathcona Park beginning in 2004, Smith had to look for creative ways to find outside funding for various projects, noting this was contrary to the public perception that taxes provided adequate financial resources for provincial parks.

The relationship with the SWI is an example of how funding relationships can work. BC Parks worked with the SWI to find funding solutions for particular projects under Andy Smith's leadership. BC Parks has matched those funds, resulting in the creation of the Centennial Loop Trail at Paradise Meadows; Battleship Lake day-use area, including a new urine diversion toilet; Croteau Lake development site; and the Strathcona Park Wilderness Centre at Paradise Meadows.[23]

The creation of the Centre began as a cooperative effort. Andy Smith led the initiative, bringing the SWI, Mt Washington Resorts and the Vancouver Island Mountain Sports Society together to find a way to secure funding for a new trailhead and centre. After several meetings a funding application was put forward but not accepted. However, Mt Washington Resorts donated land at the trailhead in 2003, for the eventuality that a centre might be built.

Five years later, Mt Washington Resorts offered the SWI a sixteen-by-twenty-square-foot ski hut, which the Institute accepted after consulting with BC Parks. The SWI committed to a fifteen-year lease with BC Parks, and funding was available from the Government Community Sustainability Trust Fund via BC Parks. Architect and mountaineer Rob Wood, a friend to the SWI, designed a two-floor plan to meet Parks specifications, a contractor was found, and work on the building began in 2009. Steve Smith wrote that the project was "a true old fashioned community effort and experience" involving local Rotarians, the FOSP, Andy Smith and Don Sharpe with Mt Washington Resorts.[24]

While the SWI is able to provide excellent visitor services at the Paradise Meadows entrance to Strathcona Park, that same service has been intermittent in the Buttle Lake corridor. Myrna Boulding, in her 1983 letter to BC Parks, outlined the challenges of a private enterprise, Strathcona Park Lodge, acting as an unofficial Parks office: "The public service by the Parks Branch doesn't excite us," she wrote, noting that the office was "rather inconspicuous," with very limited hours.[25] Although volunteers have often looked after the Buttle Lake information hut, the days and hours have been inconsistent, and there are, still today, no signs on the highway before Strathcona Lodge, telling drivers that Park information and campsites are a certain number of kilometres ahead. The hut also has no public phone.

Until 1990, some Parks personnel were present in the Buttle Lake corridor of the Park when park rangers operated out of the Buttle Lake Headquarters situated at the northeast side of Buttle Lake. The rangers maintained the "frontcountry," twelve trailheads and toilet facilities, and looked after the Buttle Lake and Ralph River campsites, as well as five marine campsites. Elizabeth Purkiss, who began working as a ranger at Buttle Lake in 1987, was offered the opportunity to contract these services to BC Parks when her position ended in 1990. She and her former Parks colleague Dave Fairhurst worked as partners in the business, and hired seasonal employees. She found it very busy, and on top of the physical work of maintaining the frontcountry, she often answered campers' and hikers' questions about the park. Purkiss left in 2003 to take various supervisory positions as a Parks employee in the BC Interior, then returned in 2015 to the Miracle Beach Parks Headquarters, where she worked with Andy Smith and managed contracts for mid- and north Vancouver Island until her retirement in 2020.[26]

Today, 43K Wilderness Solutions holds the contract to operate in Strathcona Park and at Cape Scott Provincial Park, both front and backcountry. They note on their website that "the geographically dispersed, remote locations of Strathcona's recreation sites makes for challenging logistics. Careful planning, an organised procurement process and staff well-versed at working in isolated conditions are essential for our success."[27]

Access to the Wilderness

Despite the availability of expert and often professional advice, visitors to the Park in recent years often take unnecessary and frequently fatal risks when using the wilderness. In 2020, a hiker from Black Creek, BC, Laurence Philippsen, who was considered to be experienced and well equipped, entered Strathcona Park with the ambitious agenda of climbing three different mountain peaks on a solo expedition, in a rugged area that required technical expertise. He left June 20 and was expected to return July 2. He disappeared without a trace for several months, even though he had gone in with the best communication equipment for backcountry travel. Comox Valley Search & Rescue suspended the search when "no clues were produced to lead us to Laurence's whereabouts amidst this rugged and remote area of Vancouver Island."[28] Philippsen's friends persisted, and his body was located on the south side of Mt Laing on August 20. Lindsay Elms, a friend of Philippsen, said it appeared that he fell and died instantly. "As mountaineers, we know only too well that there is this side to mountaineering," wrote Elms in a social media post. "There is passion, but also pain. I will remember Laurence for many things, but it was his love of adventure and his willingness to explore new places that brought us together in the mountains."[29]

Jamie Boulding, Director of Strathcona Park Lodge, commented that Philippsen's agenda was ambitious and said that he believes those attempting difficult climbs should always travel in threes.[30]

The experience of front line staff at Strathcona Park Lodge is that numerous visitors to the Park read online blogs that often exaggerate the ease of accessing or tackling certain trails, waterfalls or climbs. A common request is for directions to Della Falls from the Buttle Lake corridor, indicating that the potential visitor has conducted little or no research into how to access the falls. When Myrna Boulding worked in the office, she would often advise visitors to "fly over the falls" rather than make the arduous trip via Great Central Lake outside Port Alberni. Della Falls, as Philip Stone notes in *Exploring Strathcona Park*, is sought out more often by visitors to British Columbia rather than by locals for its reputation as the highest waterfall in Canada, as many British Columbians are aware of numerous other spectacular falls more easily accessible.[31] The most recent Strathcona Park brochure categorizes the hike to Della Falls as difficult. "In the backcountry, adventurous visitors can see the beautiful Della Falls, whose drop of 440 metres over three cascades makes it one of the highest waterfalls in Canada. (Note—this remote area is not regularly maintained and is difficult to access)."[32]

Access to the falls has, despite their popularity, changed little since Joe Drinkwater first travelled the area, and the trip is not easy. The trail from the head of Great Central Lake to the base of the falls is described in *Hiking Trails III* as sixteen kilometres long, taking seven hours one way.[33] The trip across the lake has the potential to be hazardous. "Regardless," writes Stone, "the setting of Della Falls at the head of the verdant Drinkwater Valley surrounded by the summits and glaciers of Mt Rosseau, Nine Peaks and Big Interior Mountain is outstanding."[34]

Another popular excursion is to Mt Albert Edward near Mt Washington. In recent years the idea of climbing this mountain as a day trip has increased in popularity, resulting in an increase in the number of rescues performed by local Search and Rescue (SAR) organizations of ill-equipped and uninformed hikers. Stories abound of hikers dressed in summer clothing, without adequate provisions or extra clothing, attempting the climb and either getting lost or having to give up when inclement weather has rolled in. Andy Smith describes the climb as an "unmaintained route in a wilderness area" and notes that many "at risk" visitors are attempting this climb, assuming that it is a "nice well marked trail, much like the trails throughout the plateau area."[35]

To help mitigate the number of people requiring rescue, BC Parks has consulted with local SAR reps and come up with a plan to enhance safety. Guide markers have been erected at Jutland Ridge to guide hikers descending the mountain during white-out conditions. New signage explaining safety precautions and what to do and not do will be erected at the head of the route. BC Parks intends to complement this information with a website where potential hikers can access a downloadable route map.

Myrna Boulding has always thought BC Parks should register the trips of hikers. Andy Smith, however, has explained that "there is only so much BC Parks can take responsibility for." He feels that after BC Parks ensures facilities are safe and functional, tags potential hazards and posts advisories on their website, "safety must move to the visitor."[36]

Another safety and visitor challenge is monitoring snowmobilers' access to the Park. Because the boundaries are so awkward, especially where there is remote logging road access toward Gold River off Highway 28, and where the boundaries are close to popular spots such as Mt Washington, Smith says BC Parks is working on new enforcement strategies. Ideally, he would like to see winter programming for the Park with winter hosts.[37]

BC Parks is also challenged with its own access to certain areas of Strathcona Park, where the Park borders on logging property. Smith is required to request a key from logging companies such as Mosaic to unlock gates that restrict his entry; conversely, companies are required to contact him when they will be logging up to Park boundaries. In these matters there is ongoing compromise, certainly not foreseen by McBride when he created the boundaries in 1910.

With Myra Falls mining operations there is excellent communication. In fact, Smith relates that they "communicate everything." Having worked in mining himself, he is aware of mining protocols and is able to discuss best methods of mitigating environmental damage.

Smith enjoys being part of the SPPAC, which he says provides an important service and allows him to speak as an individual, outside of his role as Park Supervisor. He also feels that because Parks employees are not often in a position to effect change, it is important for the public to voice their opinions. Gone are the heady days of 1980s activism, when it took a concerted effort on the part of the public and a high profile protest to alter the British Columbia government's long-standing acceptance of multiple use in its wilderness parks. This endeavour was successful, and opened the door for a more cooperative style of park management.

Smith feels that Park administration today faces a dual mandate: to conserve, while assisting the public to enjoy recreation in parks. To achieve this it is often necessary to alter the landscape, even if a portion of the public would prefer that wilderness areas remain untouched and pristine.[38]

While not all users and lovers of Strathcona Park may agree on changes in the Park, the SWI stands out as an example of what a cooperative effort can achieve. Working with BC Parks and the Friends of Strathcona Park, the SWI has emerged as an organization that exemplifies stewardship of the wilderness, through providing interpretation and doing research into the natural world that can be used to educate the public, which ultimately protects both people and the environment.

CONCLUSION
The Legacy of Myra Falls Mine and a Look at the Future of the Park

A SENSE OF PLACE develops by travelling the roadways, fishing the rivers, walking in the woods and drinking the waters of a specific locality. And nobody knew that better than Vancouver Island conservationist Roderick Haig-Brown, who frequently expressed his own sense of place. His feelings and values were reflected in the simple, rural lifestyle the writer created for himself and his family on the outskirts of Campbell River beginning in the 1930s. Those such as Haig-Brown who have explored and been neighbours to Strathcona Provincial Park have keenly felt the losses that have resulted from the Park's exploitation by logging, mining and hydro-electric interests. Haig-Brown's was not a lone voice in the wilderness speaking out against degradation of the Park; conservationist Will Reid; the nearest neighbours to the Park, Jim and Myrna Boulding; members of the FOSP; and Comox Valley environmentalist Ruth Masters have been vocal about their desire to protect the Park's wilderness values, as have mountaineers Rob Wood, Lindsay Elms and Philip Stone. Campbell River logging operator Wallace Baikie, a contemporary of Haig-Brown, cared enough to produce a book about its history.

As an area recognized for its exceptional beauty, the Park was established in 1911 with the intent that it would be set aside "for the enjoyment of the people."[1] This was followed by eighty years of differing views over how to utilize its natural resources, with escalating discontent from the public over exclusion from the decisions that affected the future of the Park.

Writing in 1992, John Dwyer believed the successes of the FOSP would be short-lived and industry would prevail in BC's parks and protected spaces.[2] He could not have known that the Master Plan would protect the Park from industrial development and that the SWI, rather than taking on an activist role, would instead work to educate and serve the public, and solve issues together with BC Parks.

In 2009, Strathcona Park Lodge celebrated its fiftieth anniversary, reuniting founder Myrna Boulding with many former staff, a number of whom, such as the Smiths, Rob Wood, Jim Rutter, Ann Fiddick, Karen Schwalm and Teresa Strukoff, participated in the events of the late 1980s and early '90s. When I later contacted them and told them about my intentions to write their stories, they were pleased that I would "set the record straight." I hope that I have achieved that here.

Strathcona Park Lodge has an ongoing relationship with the Park, providing park information to passing tourists and guests, and using the Park for its programs, most notably Canadian Outdoor Leadership Training (COLT). Buttle Lake water today is considered safe for human consumption. Trout are present in both Buttle and Upper Campbell Lakes, as well as in the Elk River, although populations will likely never rebound to the numbers prior to the Myra Falls mine going in. Acid mine waste is currently treated, but what will happen when, one day, the mine closes? Dr. Tom Pedersen considers that the waste dump at the mine is a "time bomb" that will exist for centuries to come. He also contends that the tailings ponds are another source of sulphuric acid and is concerned about the consequences of an earthquake in this seismically sensitive zone.[3]

Strathcona Provincial Park, British Columbia's oldest park, has two legacies to take it into the future: a legacy of misuse and permanent damage, accompanied by one of hope and human concern for ensuring that this outstanding wilderness area will continue to bring special experiences for future generations.

ACKNOWLEDGEMENTS

MANY PEOPLE and organizations are involved in bringing a project of this nature to fruition, and it is difficult to know where to begin in order to thank everyone who contributed to the undertaking. However, since much of the inspiration for writing this history came from my relationship with Strathcona Park Lodge and Outdoor Education Centre and from being physically near the Park, I will begin by thanking Myrna Boulding, who is a dear friend with whom I have worked in several capacities over the years, beginning in 1981. Her constant faith that I could undertake and complete any project I worked on, and her belief in me as a writer, has in many ways made this possible, as has her enthusiasm for the fact that I was writing about the Park, a place both near and dear to her.

I also appreciate the support and enthusiasm of Strathcona Park Lodge staff both past and present, including Myrna's son Jamie Boulding, with whom I have had many stimulating conversations, and his wife and co-director of the Lodge Christine Clarke.

My dear friend Teresa Strukoff first told me about the 1988 protests in the Park in the early 2000s. She sparked my interest in that story, which led to my interviewing her and other old Strathcona friends and former colleagues Karen Schwalm and Ann Fiddick. Jim Rutter, another old "Lodgie," was extremely helpful, and, of course, so were Marlene and Steve Smith, who continue to support and care for the Park, and who were at the forefront of the important changes brought about in the late 1980s. Suzanne Lawson provided me with substantial files on Strathcona Park, which have been enormously helpful. The work of Lindsay Elms, Philip Stone and Rob Wood, all former "Lodgies" and mountaineers, who wrote about the Park before me and continue to be enthusiastic about its history, has been absolutely invaluable.

Thanks to Hardolph Wasteneys, who resides at Strathcona Lodge and has been on the Strathcona Park Public Advisory Committee for many years, who suggested I speak with Dr. Tom Pedersen about acid mine drainage.

I would also like to thank my friends and former colleagues at the Museum at Campbell River, Executive Director Sandra Parrish and Collections Manager Megan Purcell, for their assistance in procuring images for this book and for their ongoing support and interest in what I'm working on. Thanks, too, to Curator Beth Boyce for a consultation.

Thanks to Catherine Siba at the Courtenay and District Museum and Archives, who kindly assisted me with gathering information on Forbidden Plateau.

Thanks to Dorothy Hunt, Lands Manager with the Mowachaht/ Muchalaht First Nation (MMFN) in Gold River, and Sheila Savey Sr., Researcher MMFN in Evidence Gathering.

And thanks to Chuck Symes, a "history friend" and Heritage Interpreter in Gold River, whose enthusiasm and assistance I truly value.

Bill Merilees has been extremely helpful in procuring information on BC Parks and past employees, and providing me with leads that were well worth following up. His extensive interviews with BC Parks employees are an important resource for anyone who wishes to understand the history of that organization.

Betty Brooks wrote a 1989 report on Strathcona Park that has been an excellent resource, as has her personal history with the Comox District Mountaineering Club and Strathcona Wilderness Institute. Betty's pictures of Forbidden Plateau are a wonderful addition to that story.

Thank you to Andy Smith, the Strathcona Park Area Supervisor, who has been supportive, informative and enthusiastic about having the Park's history made available.

Joe Bordeville, with whom discussions were begun on Will Reid, introduced me to Reid's family and has generously shared his research.

Members of the Will J. Reid family have been extremely generous in offering historical material about Reid's history and continue as trustees, all volunteers, with the Reid Foundation, whose main work is charitable distributions. The founders of the Reid Foundation include Will J. Reid, Ella Hancock Reid, Virginia Hancock Reid, Wm. T. Hancock (Will Hancock's father) and Charles Reid Gaylord (son of Will J. Reid's sister). A very special thanks to Foundation Trustee Will Hancock, who assembled, copied and sent by mail the thousand pages of minutes from the 1951 hearings pertaining to the damming of Buttle Lake, a part of the "History of the Founders" collection, at the Foundation's expense. I would like to express a special thanks to Reid's granddaughter Elizabeth Westbrook, President of the Foundation, whose overall assistance has been most treasured. Elizabeth scanned and assembled her mother Virginia's many photos of Buttle Lake, developed and printed in her mother's own darkroom, that offer a personal glimpse into life at the lake in the 1930s, '40s and '50s.

Owen Grant, of Baseline Archaeology, has graciously allowed me to tell of his archaeological finds at Buttle Lake.

Dr. Richard Rajala, now retired professor of BC Environmental History at the University of Victoria, was my supervisor when I wrote my thesis. His willingness to take me on, his meticulous appraisal of my paper, and his insightful criticisms and suggestions led me to look into new and wonderful places. Much of this research formed the basis of this book.

Thanks to my daughter, Renee Reedel, who helped pull together some of the final touches of the manuscript.

Editor Audrey McClellan, with her keen eye, did an amazing job finding all the errors and omissions in the manuscript, and made excellent suggestions. Thanks also to the team at Heritage House Publishing for their work turning the manuscript into a book and for all the support throughout.

And, of course, thank you to all my family, who are supportive and believe in what I do, and who simply think to ask me how I am.

TOP Schjelderup Lake. JIM RUTTER COLLECTION

BOTTOM Rambler Peak. PHILIP STONE

ABOVE Arrowheads found at Buttle Lake in 2019. COURTESY OWEN GRANT

OPPOSITE A microblade core found at Buttle Lake. COURTESY OWEN GRANT

OPPOSITE, TOP Black bears are often seen in the park. ROBERT FRASER

OPPOSITE, BOTTOM Roosevelt elk can be seen on the flats in the Elk River Valley. PHILIP STONE

TOP Trumpeter swan. ROBERT FRASER

BOTTOM Vancouver Island marmot. RYAN TIDMAN COURTESY MARMOT RECOVERY FOUNDATION

OPPOSITE An alpine meadow. PHILIP STONE

ABOVE From the summit of the Golden Hinde, looking north to Victoria Peak, the Elkhorn and Mt Colonel Foster. JIM RUTTER COLLECTION

OPPOSITE, TOP A colourized image of beautiful Della Lake. IMAGE PN0066
ALBERNI VALLEY MUSEUM PHOTOGRAPH COLLECTION

OPPOSITE, BOTTOM At Upper Campbell Lake, looking into the Elk River
Valley, 1948. PAINTING BY ALBERT ROLAND DAVIDSON, ANN FIDDICK COLLECTION

ABOVE Paradise Meadows. JOE MCCARTHY

ABOVE Seal of the Comox District Mountaineering Club. BETTY BROOKS COLLECTION

OPPOSITE, TOP Baby Bedwell Lake in the Bedwell Valley. TERESA STRUKOFF

OPPOSITE, BOTTOM Jim Rutter at the summit of Mt Colonel Foster. JIM RUTTER COLLECTION

Don't CUT THE ♥ OUT OF STRATHCONA PARK

TOP FOSP strategic meeting, 1987. From left to right: Kel Kelly, Peggy Carswell, Colleen McRory (on chair), Carol Latter, Walter Latter (behind her), Tom Black, Sharon Black, Marlene Smith. MARLENE SMITH COLLECTION

BOTTOM FOSP slogan. MYRNA BOULDING COLLECTION

OPPOSITE, TOP Teresa Strukoff hiking in Strathcona Park, early 1980s. MYRNA BOULDING COLLECTION

OPPOSITE, BOTTOM Karen Schalm with a whiskey jack, early 1980s. KAREN SCHWALM COLLECTION

ABOVE Blockade at Cream Silver site in Strathcona Park, 1988. MARLENE SMITH COLLECTION

OPPOSITE Ruth Masters (centre) at Bedwell Trail bridge, 1998. MARLENE SMITH COLLECTION

ABOVE Paradise Meadows. VIKTOR DAVARE

OPPOSITE, TOP Strathcona Wilderness Institute information centre under construction. COURTESY ALISON MAINGON

OPPOSITE, BOTTOM The information centre, completed. KRISTA KAPTEIN

TOP Buttle Lake. EMMA HAY

BOTTOM A group of participants awaiting a guided hike in front of the SWI Infocentre. ALISON MAINGON

OPPOSITE Flowers at Marble Meadows. EMMA HAY

OPPOSITE, TOP Lower Myra Falls. EMMA HAY

OPPOSITE, BOTTOM Marlene and Steve Smith at Carey Lakes. BETTY BROOKS COLLECTION

ABOVE Landslide Lake, 1970. MYRNA BOULDING COLLECTION

ABOVE Lupines in Marble Meadows. EMMA HAY

OPPOSITE Castlecrag Mountain. JOE MCCARTHY

OPPOSITE Lake and mountain view. JIM RUTTER

ABOVE Night view south into Buttle Lake. ROBERT FRASER

OPPOSITE Mountain meadow. JIM RUTTER

TOP Karen Schwalm on the Elk River Trail Traverse. KAREN SCHWALM COLLECTION

BOTTOM Septuagenarian hiking group honouring Roderick Haig-Brown, circa 2007. From left to right: Bill Baillergeon, Mary Haig-Brown, Valerie Haig-Brown, guide Philip Stone, Justin Bennett, guide from Strathcona Lodge and Brian Gunn. PHILIP STONE COLLECTION

TOP Paradise Meadows in 2020. VIKTOR DAVARE

BOTTOM Glacier-fed lake. JIM RUTTER

OPPOSITE Looking at Mt McBride. EMMA HAY

TOP Mariwood Lake area view to Castlecrag. DAVE FAIRHURST COLLECTION

BOTTOM Firewood for the Buttle Lake and Ralph River campsites.
DAVE FAIRHURST COLLECTION

TIMELINE OF STRATHCONA PROVINCIAL PARK HISTORY

1865 Commander John James Buttle led the first exploratory expedition of Europeans into the area from Bedwell Sound where gold was discovered. Buttle Lake is named after him, but it is now thought he was viewing Great Central Lake.

1892 Michael and James King, American entrepreneurs and explorers, crossed through the area that was to become the Park. Although mainly interested in the hydro-electric potential of the Campbell River watershed, they drew attention to the interior region's magnificent mountains.

1986 Reverend William Bolton and his group explored several areas in central Vancouver Island that had not yet been seen by earlier explorers.

1909 A survey was conducted of the E & N land grant that led to a subsequent survey of the newly formed Strathcona Reserve. In Victoria, interest groups began to urge the provincial government to consider attracting tourists to Vancouver Island.

1910 An expedition was undertaken at the request of Premier Richard McBride to decide if the region explored by Bolton was suitable as a wilderness park. Led by Chief Commissioner of Lands Price Ellison, the party numbered twenty-three, and included Ellison's daughter Myra, local guide "Lord" Bacon, William Bolton, First Nations guides from Duncan, surveyors, a photographer and a journal keeper.

1911 Price Ellison wrote a glowing report which resulted in provincial protection of the area by the Strathcona Park Act. A triangle with Crown Mountain at its northern tip, the line marking the E & N land grant created its eastern border, and straight lines drawn through the western Pacific side and southern area near Great Central Lake formed the other two boundaries. The park was made up of 524,000 acres and was named after Donald Alexander Smith, 1st Baron Strathcona.

1912 Construction began on a road from Campbell River toward the Buttle Lake entrance to the Park.

1913 The boundaries of the park were surveyed by W.J.H. Holmes, and roads were built around Buttle Lake.

1916 The government published *Strathcona the Beautiful* to advertise the "Vancouver Island Alps." In that same year, road construction ended due to the government's focus on the First World War.

1918 The Park Act was amended to open Strathcona up for mineral claims. While this solved the issue of the province having to purchase the claims that existed at the time of the Park's inception, it resulted in more than 400 additional claims being staked.

1925 Forbidden Plateau (which would not be annexed to the Park until 1967) was being publicized by Clinton Wood and Ben Hughes of the Comox Valley for its recreational values.

1927 The Strathcona Park Act was amended once more to allow water levels to be raised in Buttle and four other lakes when Crown Willamette expressed an interest in harnessing hydro-electric power for the purpose of powering a pulp and paper mill.

1929 Many timber licences that existed at the time of the Park's formation were purchased by the provincial government around the Buttle Lake area, but some remained in the Elk River, Ash River and Drinkwater Creek areas.

1939 A logging railway was constructed up Drinkwater Creek to the gold mine.

1945 The BC Power Commission was established, and its first local project was the John Hart Dam at Elk Falls, creating a reservoir of the Campbell River, which became known as John Hart Lake. Subsequently, in 1949, Ladore Falls was dammed at Lower Campbell Lake. Trees were left standing, creating a mess at the lake.

1951 The BC Power Commission proposed building a dam at Buttle Lake. Intense public pressure ensued, resulting in a series of hearings. Roderick Haig-Brown was highly vocal against the proposition.

1955 The damsite was moved to the northeast side of Upper Campbell Lake. Before flooding of the valley, trees were cleared. Water levels rose significantly in both Upper Campbell and Buttle Lakes, as well as into the Elk River Valley. Trees as large as seventeen feet in diameter were removed from the Elk River Valley. Bloedel, Stewart and Welch received cutting rights in the Ash River area.

1957 The Strathcona Park Act was repealed and responsibility for the Park removed from the Department of Forests and passed to the Department of Recreation and Conservation. The area was reclassified as a Class A park.

1958 A forest fire burned approximately 2,000 hectares in the Thelwood Creek area at the south end of Buttle Lake. Salvage logging was permitted.

1959 A revision in the Park Act allowed Western Mines to begin establishing a mine at the south end of Buttle Lake. Blocks 122 to 126 at Buttle Lake were added to the Park.

1961 Western Mines, later called Westmin, received permission to activate its claims (established in 1925) on Lynx, Myra and Price Creeks. Open-pit mining commenced in the park.

1962 The Bedwell Valley was reclasssified as Class B park (allowing for industry) and sections of the lower valley were logged by MacMillan Bloedel, allowing BC Parks to purchase certain company holdings. The Strathcona timber was exchanged for property in Pacific Rim National Park, Shawnigan and Bowron Lakes, Island View Beach, Kokanee Creek and De Courcy Island.

    In the same year, BC Hydro (formerly the BC Power Commission) commenced blasting a channel from Burman Lake to the Wolf River basin to provide additional water flow into Buttle Lake without Parks permission.

1963 A transmission line was constructed from the Strathcona Dam, at the northeast end of Upper Campbell Lake, along the west side of the lake, then turning west at the Elk River Valley to where the line parallels the Elk River all the way to Gold River. The line passes through Park land and was built to power the new pulp mill at Gold River and the village.

    Westmin dammed Tennent Lake to provide power for its mine as BC Hydro would not build lines along Buttle Lake to the mine site. Water was siphoned from many lakes around Tennent, outside of the Westmin claim, as a result.

1964 Minister of Recreation and Conservation Kenneth Kiernan allowed Western Mines to improve a twenty-two-mile access road that followed along the east side of Buttle Lake. This road was partly funded by provincial money.

1965 Strathcona Park was reclassified from Class A to Class B status by order-in-council to permit mining. Roughly half of the Park's acreage was set aside as a Nature Conservancy area.

1967 Cream Silver Mines registered mineral claims along Price Creek and around Cream Lake and over the next three years received permission to explore and drill. Pamela Creek and Burman River areas were exchanged for Rathtrevor Beach near Parksville.

1967 Forbidden Plateau, an area of 30,680 acres was added to the park in a land swap with Pacific Logging (a subsidiary of CPR), which in exchange received 20,000 acres in the Robertson Valley on the south side of Cowichan Lake. Block 1012 at Buttle Lake was added to the Park.

1969 Two hundred acres of land near the Buttle Lake bridge was obtained from BC Hydro. Part of the Park east of Buttle Lake was reclassified as Class A. Timber rights at Gretchen Creek, Ranald Creek and Oshinow Lake areas were logged in exchange for land at Cape Scott. Raven Lumber received 5,260 acres of Strathcona forest for 576 acres of the northern tip of Vancouver Island in what the government called "a fair swap."

1973 With a change in government, a moratorium was placed on further prospecting and staking of claims in the park. At the same time, Westmin received permission to dump mine tailings into Buttle Lake.

1980 Westmin mines applied for a major expansion, prompting a study of Buttle Lake water quality. Biologist Malcolm

Clark reported in 1982 that copper and zinc were present in Buttle Lake and posed a threat to aquatic life.

The Gold Lake area at the northwest corner of the Park was added.

1982 A further study of water quality was launched, which recognized that acid waste from the mine site flowed into Myra Creek and the lake, endangering the health of fish.

1985 Permission was granted to dam Jim Mitchell Lake for the purpose of generating additional electrical power for Westmin. A road was built up to the lake. Deputy Parks Minister Vince Collins signed Park Use Permit No. 1363, which gave Westmin sole and exclusive right to 6,249 acres of land in Strathcona for twenty-five years for a paltry sixty dollars per year.

1985 The provincial government appointed a Wilderness Advisory Committee (WAC) to examine wilderness areas, including Strathcona Park. The Park celebrated its seventy-fifth anniversary.

Westmin was fined $80,000 for destruction of fish habitat based on the 1982 report.

1986 The WAC recommended that 87,500 acres be deleted from Strathcona Park and that 20,000 acres be added, and recommended that the central portion be reclassified as "Recreation Area" so that exploitation would be uninhibited.

1987 Most WAC recommendations were accepted without public input. An order-in-council by cabinet opened huge new areas of Strathcona Park to mining and logging. The existing freeze on resource exploration was lifted.

1988 As a result of the exploration freeze being lifted, Cream Silver mining company began exploratory drilling at its

Cream Lake site. The Friends of Strathcona Park staged a major protest in the Park against the mining company.

The Strathcona Advisory Committee was appointed in March, headed up by Peter Larkin, to review the public's opinions, with a deadline of June 30. By September, the Committee recommended no further logging or mining in the park, with the exception of Westmin. A seven member steering committee was appointed to implement the recommendations and, in the process, to begin work on a Master Plan for the Park.

1993 The Master Plan for Strathcona Park was completed and emphasized that the purpose of the Park would be for recreation. The Strathcona Park Public Advisory Committee (SPPAC), composed of members of the public, was formed.

1994 Parks budget reduced.

1995 Formation of the Strathcona Wilderness Institute.

2002 Parks budget reduced.

2010 Horse use allowed in Parks as per Master Plan 2010 amendment. A replication of the Ellison Expedition, celebrating the centennial of the 1910 Ellison Expedition, was spearheaded by Philip Stone.

2011 Strathcona Provincial Park turns 100.

2021 Strathcona Provincial Park turns 110.

NOTES

Introduction

1 The E & N land grant consisted of more than 800,000 hectares given to coal baron Robert Dunsmuir in exchange for constructing 120 kilometres of rail line on Vancouver Island in 1884. See T. Reksten, *The Dunsmuir Saga*, 61.

2 N.S. Forkey, *Canadians and the Natural Environment to the Twenty-First Century*, 3.

3 W. Guppy, *Wetcoast Ventures*, 51.

4 H. Mitchell, *Diamond in the Rough*, 128.

5 Mitchell, *Diamond in the Rough*, 128.

6 Guppy, *Wetcoast Ventures*, 51; Walter Guppy, "Mining in the Parks" (letter to the editor), *Daily Colonist*, March 9, 1965 (Lindsay Elms collection).

Chapter 1: Going Back to Where It All Began

1 J.D. Anderson, *British Columbia's Magnificent Parks*, 32–33.

2 Anderson, *British Columbia's Magnificent Parks*, 38–43.

3 T. Binnema and M. Niemi, "'Let the Line Be Drawn Now,'" 727–29.

4 J.D. Belshaw, *Canadian History*, 42–43.

5 Katie DeRosa, "Village Site on Triquet Island Proves to Be Ancient History," *Times Colonist*, April 16, 2017, https://www.timescolonist.com/news/local/village-site-on-triquet-island-proves-to-be-ancient-history-1.15548137.

6 D. Fedje et al., "A Revised Sea Level History for the Northern Strait of Georgia."

7 Owen Grant, telephone interview with Catherine Gilbert, September 1, 2020, Black Creek, BC.

8 Jesse Morin, telephone interview with Catherine Gilbert, September 25, 2020, Black Creek, BC.

9 B. Brooks, *Strathcona Provincial Park Natural and Cultural History Themes*, 15.

10 P. Stone, *Exploring Strathcona Park*, 135.

11 D.W. Nagorsen et al., *Vancouver Island Marmot Bones from Subalpine Caves*, ii.

12 Nagorsen, *Vancouver Island Marmot Bones*, 1–6.

13 *Laich-Kwil-Tach K'omoks Tlowitsis Council of Chiefs Traditional Use Project Archives*, Wei Wai Kum First Nation (Campbell River Indian Band, British Columbia) Archives.

14 Information from Sheila Savey Sr., Researcher MMFN Evidence Gathering, Gold River, BC.

15 Information from Sheila Savey Sr.

16 *Inquisition Harry Linberg Death of William McFarlane 1932*, Gold River Historical Society, Gold River, BC. Information in the next two paragraphs is from the same source.

17 Sheila Savey Sr., email correspondence, September 2020.

18 Brooks, *Strathcona Provincial Park Natural and Cultural History Themes*, 50.

19 Brooks, *Strathcona Provincial Park Natural and Cultural History Themes*, 34–35.

20 C. Scott, *Nature Strathcona*, 18.

21 Brooks, *Strathcona Provincial Park Natural and Cultural History Themes*, 15.

22 Brooks, *Strathcona Provincial Park Natural and Cultural History Themes*, 13.

23 L.J. Elms, *Beyond Nootka*, 25–26.

24 Elms, *Beyond Nootka*, 25–26; W. Guppy, *Wetcoast Ventures*, 45.

25 D.E. Isenor et al., *Edge of Discovery*, 95; Elms, *Beyond Nootka*, 31–35; P. Young, "Creating a 'Natural Asset,'" 19–22.

26 Elms, *Beyond Nootka*, 33–36.

27 Elms, *Beyond Nootka*, 65–66.

28 Guppy, *Wetcoast Ventures*, 49–50; Elms, *Beyond Nootka*, 65–66.

29 "The Passing of a Well-Known Figure: Michael King, Pioneer Timber Cruiser and Merchant Passed Away Sunday at Jubilee Hospital," *Daily Colonist*, December 20, 1910.

30 Mitchell, *Diamond in the Rough*, 81.

31 Mitchell, *Diamond in the Rough*, 128.

32 W. Baikie, with R. Philips, *Strathcona, a History*, 124.

33 Mitchell, *Diamond in the Rough*, 128.

34 Mitchell, *Diamond in the Rough*, 85–86.

35 "Passing of a Well-Known Figure."
36 Isenor, *Edge of Discovery*, 445.
37 "Passing of a Well-Known Figure."
38 Mitchell, *Diamond in the Rough*, 81–85 and 128.

Chapter 2: Why Are There No Roads into the Park?

1 Mitchell, *Diamond in the Rough*, 35.
2 W.H. Wilson, "Reginald H Thomson and Planning for Strathcona Park," 374 and 381; Elms, *Beyond Nootka*, 41; Young, "Creating a 'Natural Asset,'" 22.
3 G. Molyneux, *British Columbia*, 45–57.
4 Mid Island News Blog. "A Brief History of Nanaimo Coal," https://midislandnews.com/early-nanaimo-history/brief-history-nanaimo-coal.
5 Reksten, *Dunsmuir Saga*, 61.
6 W.A. Taylor, *Crown Land Grants*, 20.
7 Isenor, *Edge of Discovery*, 128–29.
8 H.M. Johnson, *Strathcona 1910 Discovery Expedition*, 28.
9 Quoted in Baikie, *Strathcona, a History*, 57–60.
10 Isenor, *Edge of Discovery*, 43–44.
11 Isenor, *Edge of Discovery*, 60.
12 Isenor, *Edge of Discovery*.
13 Quoted in Baikie, *Strathcona, a History*, 60.
14 Quoted in Baikie, *Strathcona, a History*, 59.
15 Baike, *Strathcona, a History*, 61.
16 L. Elms, *Price Ellison*, http://www.beyondnootka.com/biographies/ellison.html.
17 Johnson, *Strathcona 1910 Discovery Expedition*, 32
18 Johnson, *Strathcona 1910 Discovery Expedition*, 16–17.
19 Baikie, *Strathcona, a History*, 61
20 Johnson, *Strathcona 1910 Discovery Expedition*, 16 and 22.
21 Johnson, *Strathcona 1910 Discovery Expedition*, 20–22.
22 Johnson, *Strathcona 1910 Discovery Expedition*, 22.
23 P. Stone, "Introduction," in Johnson, *Strathcona 1910 Discovery Expedition*, 4.
24 T. Silkens, "The Only Lord in America," 3.
25 This and the comments from Bill Hall and Sir John Rogers are from Silkens, "The Only Lord in America," 3, 4.
26 Johnson, *Strathcona 1910 Discovery Expedition*, 16.
27 Johnson, *Strathcona 1910 Discovery Expedition*, 30.
28 Silkens, "The Only Lord in America," 4.

29 Silkens, "The Only Lord in America," 4.

30 Johnson, *Strathcona 1910 Discovery Expedition*, 69.

31 Johnson, *Strathcona 1910 Discovery Expedition*, 110.

32 Johnson, *Strathcona 1910 Discovery Expedition*, 123.

33 Johnson, *Strathcona 1910 Discovery Expedition*, 131.

34 Johnson, *Strathcona 1910 Discovery Expedition*, 143–59.

35 Anderson, *British Columbia's Magnificent Parks*, 50.

36 Guppy, *Wetcoast Ventures*, 51; Young, "Creating a 'Natural Asset,'" 22.

37 D.M. Trew, *Reconnaissance Report on Strathcona Park*, 3.

38 Mitchell, *Diamond in the Rough*, 45 and 131.

39 Isenor, *Edge of Discovery*, 187; *Strathcona News* (Spring 1988), 6; Anderson, *British Columbia's Magnificent Parks*, 51.

40 An editorial in *Comox Argus*, March 21, 1918, quoted in Isenor, *Edge of Discovery*, 187.

41 M.C. Holmes, *Reginald H. Thomson*.

42 Wilson, "Reginald H. Thomson," 377–78.

43 Wilson, "Reginald H. Thomson."

44 Mitchell, *Diamond in the Rough*, 35–36.

45 R.H. Thomson, *Third Annual Progress Report*, 17.

46 Eric Sismey, "Eric Sismey Helped Survey Strathcona Park in 1912," *Daily Colonist*, May 12, 1968 (Lindsay Elms collection).

47 Baikie, *Strathcona, a History*, 75–80; Thomson, *Third Annual Progress Report*, 14.

48 Baikie, *Strathcona, a History*, 75–80.

49 Sismey, "Eric Sismey Helped Survey Strathcona Park in 1912."

50 Wilson, "Reginald H. Thomson," 380.

51 "Scenic Attractions Strathcona Park" (editorial), *Daily Colonist*, April 26, 1914; Johnson, *Strathcona 1910 Discovery Expedition*, 125.

52 Baikie, *Strathcona, a History*, 75–80; Wilson, "Reginald H. Thomson," 383.

53 Michael Dawson has discussed early twentieth century boosterism in BC and the lead role Cuthbert took in promoting Victoria and the Island to tourists, settlers and investors in *Selling British Columbia*, 26–37.

54 "Cannot Develop Strathcona Park" (editorial), *Daily Colonist*, November 20, 1915.

55 "Cannot Develop Strathcona Park."

56 "Cannot Develop Strathcona Park"; B. Waiser, *Park Prisoners*.

57 *Strathcona the Beautiful, Canada's Unrivalled National Park* is reproduced in B. Tustin, *History of Mountaineering on Vancouver Island*.

58 "Island's Finest Beauty Spots," *Daily Colonist*, May 25, 1919.

59 "Better Roads Would Do Much for Island," *Daily Colonist*, February 26, 1922.

60 Quoted in Baikie, *Strathcona, a History*, 87.

61 Quoted in Baikie, *Strathcona, a History*, 71–73.

62 "Opening Up Strathcona Park," *Comox Argus*, August 14, 1924, and "Want Strathcona Park Road at Once," *Comox Argus*, October 11, 1925, reproduced in Baikie, *Strathcona, a History*, 87–90.

63 "Park Development," *Daily Colonist*, June 2, 1926.

64 Anderson, *British Columbia's Magnificent Parks*, 61.

65 Department of Lands, *Strathcona Park, Vancouver Island*, 3.

66 "Island Roads Tithe of Mainland Work," *Daily Colonist*, May 17, 1936, 5.

67 Frank M. Kelley, "Strathcona Provincial Park," *Daily Colonist*, November 14, 1944.

68 Anderson, *British Columbia's Magnificent Parks*, 60.

69 Knewstubb quoted in "Minutes of Proceedings at Hearings Re: Application to Water Rights Branch," 756–57.

70 Anderson, *British Columbia's Magnificent Parks*, 60.

71 Mitchell, *Diamond in the Rough*, 49.

72 "Minutes of Proceedings at Hearings," 900.

73 Baikie, *Strathcona, a History*, 80–81; Baikie notes that the public preferred the logging road built by Elk River Timber. Isenor, *Edge of Discovery*, 252.

74 Baikie, *Strathcona, a History*, 82.

75 Trew, *Reconnaissance Report*, 3.

76 Trew, *Reconnaissance Report*, 4.

77 R. Haig-Brown, "Strathcona Park and Buttle Lake, Our Only Living Museum," *Victoria Times*, June 20, 1951; John Dwyer notes that relief workers improved the trail to Buttle Lake in 1933, see "Conflicts Over Wilderness," 105. For a comprehensive article on relief workers in the Depression years, see R. Rajala, "From 'On-to-Ottawa' to 'Bloody Sunday,'" 118–50.

78 Haig-Brown, "Strathcona Park and Buttle Lake."

79 Mary Haig-Brown, interview with Catherine Gilbert, January 28, 2018, Victoria.

80 See R. Rajala, "'Streams Being Ruined."

81 Anderson, *British Columbia's Magnificent Parks*, 67–68.

82 Anderson, *British Columbia's Magnificent Parks*, 80.

83 Chester Lyons, interview with Bill Merilees, Tape 4A, October 14, 1996, from series of taped interviews conducted with former Parks employees from 1997 to 2008.

Chapter 3: Loggers, Trespassers and Millionaires

1 W. Baikie, *Rolling with the Times*, 129.
2 Baikie, *Rolling with the Times*, 129–32.
3 Myrna Boulding and Joanne Campbell, interview with Catherine Gilbert, August 10, 2020, Campbell River.
4 M. Boulding, *Surviving Strathcona Style*, 3 and 4.
5 Trew, *Reconnaissance Report*, 44–47.
6 "Buttle Lake by Flying Boat, Fishing Party Catches Scenery," *Sunday Province*, no date on copy (Will J. Reid Foundation Founders' History Collection).
7 Brooks, *Strathcona Provincial Park Natural and Cultural History Themes*, 130.
8 Ronald E. Park, "Scot from Finland Evaded Czar's Yoke," *Vancouver Sun*, September 20, 1947 (Will J. Reid Foundation Founders' History Collection).
9 "Opening Up Resort at Buttle's Lake," *Nanaimo Daily News*, June 24, 1932 (Joe Bordeville Collection).
10 "Buttle Lake by Flying Boat, Fishing Party Catches Scenery."
11 Camp Alicia Guestbook (Will J. Reid Foundation Founders' History Collection).
12 James Hancock, interview with Catherine Gilbert, May 30, 2020, Black Creek.
13 Hancock interview.
14 Hancock interview.
15 Correspondence between Will J. Reid and Roderick Haig-Brown, 1939–1956, University of British Columbia Library Rare Books and Special Collections (Will J. Reid Foundation Founders' History Collection).
16 Correspondence between Will J. Reid and Roderick Haig-Brown.
17 "Minutes of Proceedings at Hearings," 877.
18 Anderson, *British Columbia's Magnificent Parks*, 80.

Chapter 4: "The Battle for Buttle": Canada's First Environmental Conflict

1 "Rebuttle by Power Commission," *Victoria Times*, September 25, 1951; "Permission to Dam Buttle Lake," *Victoria Times*, November 7, 1951; H. Baikie, *A Boy and His Axe*, 56–57; Isenor, *Edge of Discovery*, 161.
2 Dwyer, "Conflicts Over Wilderness," 113–15; *Comox Argus*, June 13, 1951. Haig-Brown was particularly critical of the province's multiple-use

philosophy for parks; see R. Rajala, "'Nonsensical and a Contradiction in Terms.'"

3   *Comox Argus*, June 13, 1951.

4   A. Nikiforuk, "Why We Need Haig-Brown More Than Ever," 22; Y. Qureshi, "Environmental Issues in British Columbia," 97–102.

5   Grant Shilling, "Ruth Masters... Visions of Paradise, Eekology, Snafus, Boners and Belly Laughs," *The GIG*, April/May 2000; Judy Hagen, "Ruth Masters, the Passing of a Vancouver Island Icon; Comox Valley Activist Dies at 97," *Comox Valley Record*, November 7, 2017.

6   Anderson, *British Columbia's Magnificent Parks*, 80–81.

7   "Minutes of Proceedings at Hearings," 29.

8   Trew, *Reconnaissance Report*, 31 and 45.

9   Correspondence between Will J. Reid and Roderick Haig-Brown.

10 Trew, *Reconnaissance Report*, 11.

11 Trew, *Reconnaissance Report*, 34–36.

12 "Sportsmen Request Reopening of Trail," *Daily Colonist*, April 5, 1950.

13 M.J.R. Clark, *Impact of Westmin Resources Ltd.*, 11; Qureshi, "Environmental Issues in British Columbia," 96.

14 Trew, *Reconnaissance Report*, 30.

15 Trew, *Reconnaissance Report*, 47.

16 Trew, *Reconnaissance Report*, 1, 3.

17 Trew, *Reconnaissance Report*, 9.

18 "Minutes of Proceedings at Hearings," 76–78.

19 "Minutes of Proceedings at Hearings," 7, 10 and 11.

20 "Minutes of Proceedings at Hearings," 48.

21 "Minutes of Proceedings at Hearings," 48.

22 "Minutes of Proceedings at Hearings," 49.

23 "Minutes of Proceedings at Hearings," 36.

24 "Minutes of Proceedings at Hearings," 697.

25 "Minutes of Proceedings at Hearings," 581.

26 "Minutes of Proceedings at Hearings," 589.

27 "Minutes of Proceedings at Hearings," 175.

28 "Minutes of Proceedings at Hearings," 877–78. Harris's testimony runs to page 897.

29 "Minutes of Proceedings at Hearings," 881.

30 "Minutes of Proceedings at Hearings," 892.

31 "Minutes of Proceedings at Hearings," 885.

32 "Minutes of Proceedings at Hearings," 897.

33 Gordon Forbes, "Buttle Lake Battle Only Started," in Myrna Boulding Collection, no identifiable date or publisher.

34 "Buttle Delay Blow to Industry," *Daily Colonist*, February 26, 1952; "Buttle Vital to Island Power," *Victoria Times*, November 21, 1952; "Power Development on Campbell River Nearing Completion," *The Province*, March 13, 1954; "Power Commission Picks Upper Campbell for Dam," *Daily Colonist*, March 5, 1955.

35 Dwyer, "Conflicts Over Wilderness," 113–15. See also T. Loo, "People in the Way."

36 Mitchell, *Diamond in the Rough*, 177.

37 C. Gilbert, "Transformation of a Town," 3.

38 Gilbert, "Transformation of a Town," 1.

39 Gilbert, "Transformation of a Town," 1.

40 "Rebuttle by Power Commission," *Victoria Times*, September 25, 1951; Baikie, *A Boy and His Axe*, 56.

41 W. Baikie, *Rolling with the Times*, 122.

42 Baikie, *A Boy and His Axe*, 56–60.

43 Mary Haig-Brown, interview with Catherine Gilbert, January 28, 2018, Victoria.

44 Haig-Brown interview.

Chapter 5: Forbidden Plateau

1 Trew, *Reconnaissance Report*, 28.

2 Brooks, *Strathcona Provincial Park Natural and Cultural History Themes*, 131.

3 Trew, *Reconnaissance Report*, 19.

4 B. Hughes, *History of the Comox Valley*, 22.

5 Rene Harding, *Daily Colonist*, April 23, 1967, in *Laich-Kwil-Tach K'omoks Tlowitsis Council of Chiefs Traditional Use Project Archives*, The Wei Wai Kum First Nation (Campbell River Indian Band, British Columbia) Archives.

6 Hughes, *History of the Comox Valley*, 11 and 12.

7 Hughes, *History of the Comox Valley*, 22.

8 Elms, *Beyond Nootka*, 24–26.

9 Brooks, *Strathcona Provincial Park Natural and Cultural History Themes*, 135.

10 Brooks, *Strathcona Provincial Park Natural and Cultural History Themes*, 136.

11 Brooks, *Strathcona Provincial Park Natural and Cultural History Themes*, 134.

12 Brooks, *Strathcona Provincial Park Natural and Cultural History Themes*, 133.

13 Doris F. Tonkin, "They Built the First Lodge on the Forbidden Plateau for the Boy Who Didn't Come Home," *Daily Colonist*, February 7, 1965.

14 C. Siba et al., *Step into Wilderness*, 49.

15 Brooks, *Strathcona Provincial Park Natural and Cultural History Themes*, 137.

16 J. Clayton, "Making Recreational Space," 77.

17 Brooks, *Strathcona Provincial Park Natural and Cultural History Themes*, 137.

18 Brooks, *Strathcona Provincial Park Natural and Cultural History Themes*, 138–40.

19 Brooks, *Strathcona Provincial Park Natural and Cultural History Themes*, 140–41.

20 Brooks, *Strathcona Provincial Park Natural and Cultural History Themes*, 141.

21 J. Clayton, "Making Recreational Space," 80.

22 Brooks, *Strathcona Provincial Park Natural and Cultural History Themes*, 141.

23 Betty Brooks, interview with Catherine Gilbert August 15, 2002, Black Creek, BC.

24 Brooks, *Strathcona Provincial Park Natural and Cultural History Themes*, 141.

25 Lindsay Elms, *Eugene Croteau*, http://www.beyondnootka.com/articles/eugene_croteau.html.

26 Brooks, *Strathcona Provincial Park Natural and Cultural History Themes*, 141.

27 Tonkin, "They Built the First Lodge on the Forbidden Plateau."

28 Tonkin, "They Built the First Lodge on the Forbidden Plateau."

29 Tonkin, "They Built the First Lodge on the Forbidden Plateau."

30 Forbidden Plateau Road Association, *History*, http://forbiddenplateauroad-association.com/history.html.

31 *Comox Argus*, October 2, 1930, found in R. Masters, "History of Forbidden Plateau."

32 *Comox Argus*, July 13, 1931, found in Masters, "History of Forbidden Plateau."

33 *Comox Argus*, July 13, 1931, found in Masters, "History of Forbidden Plateau."

34 Chester Lyons interview with Bill Merilees Tape 4A, October 14, 1996.

35 Trew, *Reconnaissance Report*, 32.

36 Trew, *Reconnaissance Report*, 33.

35 Trew, *Reconnaissance Report*.

36 *Comox Argus*, April 29, 1953, found in Masters, "History of Forbidden Plateau."

37 *Comox Argus*, August 20, 1958, found in Masters, "History of Forbidden Plateau."

38 Shilling, "Ruth Masters... Visions of Paradise, Eekology, Snafus, Boners and Belly Laughs."

39 Jenny Clayton, "From the Forbidden Plateau to Mount Washington, Skiing on Central Vancouver Island Dates to the 1920s," *Island Alpine* (July–August 2013), 12.

40 Clayton, "From the Forbidden Plateau," 12.

41 Brooks interview.

42 Clayton, "From the Forbidden Plateau," 13.

43 BC Parks, "Vancouver Island's Newest Campsite: Croteau Lake," https://
    engage.gov.bc.ca/bcparksblog/2018/04/16/vancouver-island-croteau-lake/;
    Andy Smith, interview with Catherine Gilbert, September 9, 2020, Black
    Creek, BC.

Chapter 6: A Mine in a Park?

1   Anderson, *British Columbia's Magnificent Parks*, 111.

2   Anderson, *British Columbia's Magnificent Parks*, 111.

3   Anderson, *British Columbia's Magnificent Parks*, 111.

4   Anderson, *British Columbia's Magnificent Parks*, 112.

5   Anderson, *British Columbia's Magnificent Parks*, 67–69; P. Larkin et al.,
    Strathcona Park: Restoring the Balance, 9–10.

6   Mitchell, *Diamond in the Rough*, 180–84.

7   Larkin, *Restoring the Balance*, 16.

8   Larkin, *Restoring the Balance*, 9–10; Legislative Reporter, *Daily Colonist*
    February 26, 1965; Anderson, *British Columbia's Magnificent Parks*, 69.

9   Legislative Reporter, *Daily Colonist*, February 26, 1965.

10 Isenor, *Edge of Discovery*, 185; "Western Mines Soon into Production: Old
    Claims in Strathcona Park Became Fabulous Success Story," *Upper Islander*,
    May 19, 1966.

11 Isenor, *Edge of Discovery*; Larkin, *Restoring the Balance*, 16.

12 Larkin, *Restoring the Balance*.

13 Alec Merriman, "Hunters Train Guns on Strathcona Park," *Daily Colonist*,
    September 25, 1966; Larkin, *Restoring the Balance*, 16.

14 Bob Ahrens, interview with Bill Merilees, Tape 12A, May 18, 1999.

15 Roderick Haig-Brown, "Rape of a Park," *Vancouver Sun*, March 5, 1966.

16 M. Boulding, *Survival Strathcona Style*, 2–4 and 40.

17 Myrna Boulding, interview with Catherine Gilbert, January 4, 2018,
    Campbell River, BC.

18 Baikie, *A Boy and His Axe*, 56–60; resolutions submitted by Campbell
    River and District Chamber of Commerce, Campbell River BC, Legislative
    Library of British Columbia, Victoria, BC, #333.78 C192.

19 Charlie Darkis, interview with Bill Merilees, Tape 28B, October 14, 1997.

20 "Western Mines Soon into Production," *Upper Islander*, May 19, 1966.

21 Klaus Muenter, "'Inspect Buttle Lake!' Cry Shocked Officials," *Daily
    Colonist*, February 28, 1967.

22 Boulding, *Survival Strathcona Style*, 40–44; Mitchell, *Diamond in the Rough*, 68.

23 Boulding, *Survival Strathcona Style*, 40–44.

24　Mitchell, *Diamond in the Rough*, 180.

25　"Townsite Sought by Mine Company" (editorial), *Campbell River Courier*, February 3, 1965.

26　"Game Club Joins Townsite Protest," *Vancouver Sun*, February 10, 1965.

27　Isenor, *Edge of Discovery*, 189.

28　Isenor, *Edge of Discovery*; Clark, *Impact of Westmin Resources Ltd.*, 18; "Graphic Evidence Shown in Pollution Pictures," *Campbell River Courier*, March 22, 1967.

29　Boulding, *Survival Strathcona Style*, 40; Keeling and Wynn, "The Park... Is a Mess," 137.

30　Clark, *Impact of Westmin Resources Ltd.*, 6, 36–37.

31　Boulding, *Survival Strathcona Style*, 40.

32　Clark, *Impact of Westmin Resources Ltd.*, 37; *Submission by the Campbell River District Pollution Control Society to the Pollution Control Board, concerning the addition of mine tailings into Buttle Lake, Strathcona Park, Vancouver Island* (1968), Legislative Library of British Columbia, Victoria, BC, #628.1683, 35.

33　Agnes Flett, "Nightmare of Buttle Lake," *Daily Colonist*, February 25, 1967.

34　"Water District's Appeal Is Upheld," *Campbell River Courier*, January 18, 1967.

35　Clark, *Impact of Westmin Resources Ltd.*, iii and 90.

36　Clark, *Impact of Westmin Resources Ltd.*, 37.

37　Dr. Tom Pedersen, interview with Catherine Gilbert, December 17, 2017, Victoria.

38　Clark, *Impact of Westmin Resources Ltd.*, iv and 74–75.

39　Pedersen interview. In 1983, Pedersen wrote a brief article regarding tailings behaviour in Buttle Lake, but did not discuss acid waste. See T. Pedersen, "Dissolved Heavy Metals in a Lacustrine Mine Tailings Deposit."

Chapter 7: "Don't Cut the Heart out of Strathcona Park"

1　The influx of American draft dodgers coincided with a rise in environmental activism in BC and the formation of such groups as Greenpeace, the BC Sierra Club and Society Promoting Environmental Conservation (SPEC) in the 1960s and '70s. See R. Rajala, "Forests and Fish," 92, and P. Van Huizen, "Panic Park," 73–74.

2　The Bouldings' initiative was congruent with the philosophy of American parks guru Freeman Tilden, who in 1967 wrote: "It has come to be realized that in our modern, complex world the formal education of youth in schools and colleges is not enough." F. Tilden, *Interpreting Our Heritage*, ix.

3 R. Wood, *Towards the Unknown Mountain*, 95.

4 Roger Prior, "Our 'Second Hand' Wilderness Is Living Down History Lessons," *Island Review* (June 1983), reproduced in Boulding, *Survival Strathcona Style*, 290.

5 Ann Fiddick, interview with Catherine Gilbert, December 12, 2017, Cedar BC; Jim Rutter, interview with Catherine Gilbert, November 24, 2017, Victoria.

6 Myrna Boulding, letter to Ministry of Lands, Parks and Housing, August 30, 1983, Myrna Boulding Collection.

7 Dwyer, "Conflicts Over Wilderness," 144–45; Keeling and Wynn, "The Park... Is a Mess," 140; see also Rajala, "Forests and Fish."

8 "Park Boundaries Will Change in Strathcona," *Victoria Times*, June 1, 1974.

9 *The Wilderness Mosaic* (photocopy), Susanne Lawson collection.

10 Marlene Smith, "The Birth of the Friends of Strathcona," in Boulding, *Survival Strathcona Style*, 317.

11 Wood, *Towards the Unknown Mountain*, 111.

12 Wood, *Towards the Unknown Mountain*; Smith, "The Birth of the Friends," 317.

13 Marlene and Steve Smith, interview with Catherine Gilbert, September 8, 2020, Merville BC.

14 Valhalla Society, *BC's Endangered Wilderness, A Comprehensive Proposal for Protection* (New Denver, BC: Author, 1988). For a comprehensive discussion on BC's environmental groups see J. Wilson, *Talk and Log*.

15 Marlene Smith to Susanne Lawson, March 18, 1986, Susanne Lawson collection.

16 Marlene and Steve Smith interview.

17 Wood, *Towards the Unknown Mountains*, 112; Marlene Smith, "Friends of Strathcona Park and the Strathcona Wilderness Institute," in P. Stone, *Exploring Strathcona Park*, 11. Although Dwyer, "Conflicts Over Wilderness," 141, and Keeling and Wynn, "The Park... Is a Mess," 142, cite Jim Boulding as leader and co-founder of the FOSP, he passed away before the organization was formed.

18 Quentin Dodd, "75th Anniversary of British Columbia Parks," in Baikie, *Strathcona, a History*, 126–28.

19 Marlene and Steve Smith interview.

20 Wood, *Towards the Unknown Mountains*, 112.

21 Dwyer, "Conflicts Over Wilderness," 165.

22 Susanne Lawson to the Hon. Bruce Strachan, letter dated May 7, 1986, Susanne Lawson collection.

23 Sean Griffin, "Challenging Socred Policy at Strathcona," *Pacific Tribune*, February 17, 1988, Susanne Lawson collection.

24 Lawson to Strachan, May 7, 1986.

25 BC Parks, *Striking the Balance*, 7.

26 Larkin, *Restoring the Balance*, 13.

27 "Second Mine Starts Operation in Strathcona Park Property," *Campbell River Courier*, June 14, 1967.

28 Dwyer, "Conflicts Over Wilderness," 138.

29 Isenor, *Edge of Discovery*, 192; Larkin, *Restoring the Balance*, 25; Dwyer, "Conflicts Over Wilderness," 141–44 and 152.

30 Smith, "Friends of Strathcona Park and the Strathcona Wilderness Institute," 12.

31 Teresa Strukoff, telephone interview with Catherine Gilbert, January 12, 2018, Victoria.

32 David Garrick, interview with Catherine Gilbert, October 26, 2020, Alert Bay, BC.

33 Griffin, "Challenging Socred Policy at Strathcona."

34 Strukoff interview.

35 Karen Schwalm, telephone interview with Catherine Gilbert, December 21, 2017, Campbell River BC; Strukoff interview.

36 Smith, "Friends of Strathcona Park and the Strathcona Wilderness Institute," 12.

37 "Cream Silver Meets with Residents," *Campbell River Courier*, February 18, 1988.

38 Frank Lang, (advertorial) letter from Cream Silver Mines Ltd., March 23, 1988, *Campbell River Mirror*, April 6, 1988.

39 *Strathcona News* (Spring 1988), 3.

40 Jim Rutter, interview with Catherine Gilbert, November 24, 2017, Victoria.

41 Rutter interview.

42 Rutter interview.

43 Dwyer, "Conflicts Over Wilderness," 210.

44 Submission of Dr. Bruce Wood to the hearing, Submissions 1988/Special Advisory Committee on Strathcona Park and Recreation Area, 1988, Legislative Library of British Columbia, Victoria, BC, # BC S 722 D:S8 1988, 3-4.

45 Dwyer, "Conflicts Over Wilderness," 219; BC Parks, Strathcona District, *Strathcona Provincial Park Master Plan*.

46 Rutter interview.

47 BC Parks, *Strathcona Provincial Park Master Plan*, 3.

48 Dwyer, "Conflicts Over Wilderness," 220.

49 Marlene and Steve Smith interview.

50 Fiddick interview.

51 Wood, *Towards the Unknown Mountains*, 122.

52 Fiddick interview.

53 Dwyer, "Conflicts Over Wilderness," 222–23.

54 Wood, *Towards the Unknown Mountains*, 121.

55 Jacqueline Windh, "Tofino Author Walter Guppy," *Tofino Time*, January 2005, http://www.tofinotime.com/articles/A-T501-20frm.htm.

56 BC Parks, *Strathcona Provincial Park Master Plan*, 7.

Chapter 8: Creation of a Master Plan and Contemporary History to 2020

1 BC Parks, *Strathcona Provincial Park Master Plan*, 3.

2 Philip Stone, "The Strathcona Park Advisory Committee," in Stone, *Exploring Strathcona Park*, 20.

3 Strathcona Provincial Park Advisory Committee, minutes of meeting, August 11, 2017, http://www.env.gov.bc.ca/bcparks/explore/parkpgs/strath/SPPAC/sppac-minutes-20170811.pdf?v=1521169023418.

4 Fiddick interview.

5 SPPAC, minutes of meeting, August 11, 2017; Andy Smith, email correspondence, October 11, 2020.

6 Myrna Boulding, interview with Catherine Gilbert, January 4, 2018, Campbell River, BC.

7 Ruth Masters, letter to the editor, *Comox Valley Record*, August 17, 2007.

8 Myrna Boulding, letter to BC Parks, March 17, 2008.

9 Andy Smith, interview with Catherine Gilbert, September 9, 2020, Black Creek, BC.

10 A. Smith, interview.

11 Marlene Smith, interview with Catherine Gilbert, September 8, 2020, Merville, BC.

12 Andy Smith, email correspondence, October 11, 2020.

13 A. Smith interview.

14 Ruth Masters, Editorial, *Comox Valley Record*, August 17, 2007.

15 M. Smith interview.

16 A. Smith interview.

17 M. Smith interview.

18 Boulding interview.

19 Smith, "Friends of Strathcona Park and the Strathcona Wilderness Institute," 12.

20 Steve Smith, "The Birth of the Strathcona Wilderness Institute," in P. Stone, *Exploring Strathcona Park,* 14–15.

21 Brooks interview.

22 A. Smith interview.

23 A. Smith interview.

24 Smith "The Birth of the Strathcona Wilderness Institute," 14–15.

25 Boulding, *Surviving Strathcona Style,* 271.

26 Elizabeth Purkiss, interview with Catherine Gilbert, December 22, 2020, Black Creek, BC.

27 43K Wilderness Solutions, "Case Study: Strathcona Park," https://www.43k.ca/strathcona-park.

28 Marissa Tiel, "Body of Missing Hiker Recovered near Gold River," *Campbell River Mirror,* August 26, 2020, https://www.vicnews.com/news/body-of-missing-hiker-recovered-near-gold-river.

29 Quoted in Tiel, "Body of Missing Hiker Recovered near Gold River."

30 Jamie Boulding, interview with Catherine Gilbert, August 10, 2020, Campbell River, BC.

31 Stone, *Exploring Strathcona Park,* 375.

32 BC Parks, "Strathcona Provincial Park: Park Map and Information Guide," 2019, https://bcparks.ca/explore/parkpgs/strath/strathcona_brochure.pdf?v=1608329622021.

33 Vancouver Island Trails Information Society, *Hiking Trails III,* 30.

34 Stone, *Exploring Strathcona Park,* 375.

35 A. Smith interview.

36 A. Smith interview.

37 A. Smith interview.

38 A. Smith interview.

Conclusion: The Legacy of Myra Falls Mine and a Look at the Future of the Park

1 BC Parks, *Strathcona Provincial Park Master Plan,* 5.

2 Dwyer, "Conflicts Over Wilderness," 256–60.

3 Tom Pedersen, interview with Catherine Gilbert, December 17, 2017, Victoria, BC.

BIBLIOGRAPHY

NEWSPAPER ARTICLES in the Bibliography are not cited in endnotes.

Published Materials

Anderson, James D. *British Columbia's Magnificent Parks: The First 100 Years.* Madeira Park, BC: Harbour Publishing, 2011.

Baikie, Harper. *A Boy and His Axe.* Campbell River, BC: Self-published, 1991.

Baikie, Wallace. *Rolling with the Times.* Campbell River BC: Kask Graphics, 1985.

Baikie, Wallace, with Rosemary Philips. *Strathcona, A History of British Columbia's First Provincial Park.* Campbell River BC: Ptarmigan Press, 1986.

BC Parks, Strathcona District. *Strathcona Provincial Park Master Plan.* Victoria: BC Ministry of Environment, Land and Parks, 1993 and 2001.

BC Parks. *Striking the Balance.* Victoria: BC Ministry of Environment and Parks, 1988. Susanne Lawson collection.

Belshaw, J.D. *Canadian History: Pre-Confederation.* B.C. Open Textbook Project, 2015.

Binnema, Theodore, and Melanie Niemi. "'Let the Line Be Drawn Now': Wilderness, Conservation, and the Exclusion of Aboriginal People from Banff National Park in Canada." *Environmental History* 11, no. 4 (2006): 724–50.

Boulding, Myrna. *Survival Strathcona Style: Off the Grid and on the Edge.* Campbell River, BC: Ptarmigan Press, 2009, revised 2019.

Boulding, Myrna. "Wilderness in Jeopardy: See It before It's Gone." *Campbell River Courier*, September 25, 1986.

Brooks, Betty. *Strathcona Provincial Park Natural and Cultural History Themes.* Report prepared for BC Parks, South Coast Region, North Vancouver, BC, 1989. Betty Brooks collection. Also available online at https://www.for.gov.bc.ca/hfd/LIBRARY/Documents/bib78650.pdf.

"Buttle Lake Mine Priority on Cream Silver Schedule" (editorial). *Campbell River Mirror,* July 13, 1988.

Clark, M.J.R. *Impact of Westmin Resources Ltd. Mining Operation on Buttle Lake and the Campbell River Watershed.* Vol. 1. Victoria: Ministry of Environment, Waste Management Branch, 1982. Dr. Tom Pedersen collection.

Clayton, Jenny. "Making Recreational Space: Citizen Involvement in Outdoor Recreation and Park Establishment in British Columbia, 1900–2000." PhD dissertation, University of Victoria, 2009.

Dawson, Michael. *Selling British Columbia: Tourism and Consumer Culture, 1890-1970.* Vancouver: UBC Press, 2004.

Dearden, Philip, Rick Rollins and Mark Needham, eds. *Parks and Protected Areas in Canada, Planning and Management.* 4th ed. Don Mills, ON: Oxford University Press, 2016.

Duke, David Freeland, ed. *Canadian Environmental History: Essential Readings.* Toronto: Canadian Scholars Press, 2006.

Dwyer, John M. "Conflicts over Wilderness: Strathcona Provincial Park, British Columbia." Master's thesis, Simon Fraser University, 1993.

Elms, Lindsay J. *Beyond Nootka: A Historical Perspective of Vancouver Island Mountains.* Courtenay, BC: Misthorn Press, 1996.

Eng, Paula Louise. "Parks for the People? Strathcona Park 1905–1933." Master's thesis, University of Victoria, 1996.

Fedje, Daryl, Duncan McLaren, Thomas S. James, Quentin Mackie, Nicole F. Smith, John R. Southon and Alexander P. Mackie. "A Revised Sea Level History for the Northern Strait of Georgia, British Columbia, Canada." *Quaternary Science Reviews* 192 (2018): 300–16.

Forkey, Neil S. *Canadians and the Natural Environment to the Twenty-First Century.* Toronto: University of Toronto Press, 2012.

Fry, Jack. "Richer Than Fort Knox?" *Daily Colonist,* February 25, 1965.

Gilbert, Catherine. "A Long Time Coming: Safeguarding Wilderness in Strathcona Provincial Park." Master's thesis, University of Victoria, 2018.

Gilbert, Catherine. "Transformation of a Town, the Opening of Elk Falls Pulp and Paper Mill in 1952." *Musings* 28, no. 1 (March 2009).

Guppy, Walter. "Bedwell's Booms and Busts." *The Northern Miner,* May 14, 2001. http://www.northernminer.com/news/bedwell-s-booms-and-busts/1000106408.

Guppy, Walter. *Wetcoast Ventures: Mine-Finding on Vancouver Island.* Victoria: Cappis Publishing, 1988.

Hughes, Ben. *History of the Comox Valley: 1862 to 1945.* Nanaimo: Evergreen Press, c. 1962.

Huntley, Joy. "Strange Park Gets 'Pure' Mining Townsite." *Daily Colonist,* June 10, 1966.

Isenor, Dick E., E.G. Stephens and D.E. Watson. *Edge of Discovery: A History of the Campbell River District*. Campbell River, BC: Ptarmigan Press, 1989.

Johnson, Harry McClure. *Strathcona 1910 Discovery Expedition*. Edited by Philip Stone. Quathiaski Cove, BC: WildIsle Publications, 2012.

Keeling, Arn. "A Dynamic, Not a Static Conception: The Conservation Thought of Roderick Haig-Brown." *Pacific Historical Review* 71, no. 2 (2002): 239–68.

Keeling, Arn, and Robert McDonald. "The Profligate Province: Roderick Haig-Brown and the Modernizing of British Columbia." *Journal of Canadian Studies* 36, no. 3 (2001): 7–23.

Keeling, Arn, and Graham Wynn. "'The Park... Is a Mess': Development and Degradation in British Columbia's First Park." *BC Studies* 170 (Summer 2011): 119–50.

Kelley, Frank M. "Spinal Road to Island's North Needed for Future Development." *Daily Colonist*, September 4, 1955.

Killan, Gerald. *Protected Places: A History of Ontario's Provincial Park System*. Toronto: Dundurn Press, 1993.

Larkin, Peter, Frances Jones, Roderick Nakankim and Jim Rutter (Strathcona Park Advisory Committee). *Strathcona Park: Restoring the Balance*. Victoria: Queen's Printer, June 1988.

Legislative Reporter. "Park Borders May Change But Not Acreage." *Daily Colonist*, February 26, 1965.

Loo, Tina. "People in the Way: Modernity, Environment, and Society on the Arrow Lakes." *BC Studies* 142/143 (Fall/Winter 2004/2005): 161–91.

MacEachern, Alan, and William J. Turkel, eds. *Method and Meaning in Canadian Environmental History*. Toronto: Nelson Education, 2008.

"Meeting of Alpinists." *Daily Colonist*, December 25, 1920.

Merriman, Alec. "Mr. Bennet—Move Kiernan Give Parks Post to Campbell." *Daily Colonist*, June 5, 1966.

Merriman, Alec. "Outdoors with Alec Merriman." *Daily Colonist*, March 27, 1968.

Mitchell, Helen. *Diamond in the Rough: The Campbell River Story*. Aldergrove BC: Frontier Publishing, 1966, revised 1975.

Molyneux, Geoffrey. *British Columbia: An Illustrated History*. Vancouver: Polestar Press, 1992.

Nagorsen, David W., Grant Keddie and Tanya Luszcz. *Vancouver Island Marmot Bones from Subalpine Caves: Archaeological and Biological Significance*. Occasional Paper No. 4. Victoria: Ministry of Environment, Lands and Parks, February 1996. Lindsay Elms collection. Also available online at http://bcparks.ca/conserve/occ_paper/marmot.html.

Nikiforuk, Andrew. "Why Haig-Brown Matters More Than Ever." Seventh Haig-Brown Memorial Lecture. Campbell River: Campbell River

Community Arts Council, Haig-Brown Institute, Museum at Campbell River, Pacific Wild, 2016. Available at https://www.ernstversusencana.ca/must-read-by-andrew-nikiforuk-why-haig-brown-matters-more-than-ever.

Paish, Howard. "Requiem for a Park." *BC Outdoors*, July/August 1967, 38–43.

Pedersen, Tom. "Dissolved Heavy Metals in a Lacustrine Mine Tailings Deposit—Buttle Lake, British Columbia." *Marine Pollution Bulletin* 14, no. 7 (1983): 249–54.

Qureshi, Yasmeen. "Environmental Issues in British Columbia: An Historical-Geographical Perspective." Master's thesis, University of British Columbia, 1991.

Rajala, Richard. "Forests and Fish: The 1972 Coast Logging Guidelines and British Columbia's First NDP Government." *BC Studies* 159 (2008) 81–120.

Rajala, Richard. "From 'On-to-Ottawa' to 'Bloody Sunday': Unemployment Relief and British Columbia Forests, 1935-1939." In *Framing Canadian Federalism*, eds. Dimitry Anastakis and P.E. Bryden, 118–50. Toronto: University of Toronto Press, 2009.

Rajala, Richard. "'Nonsensical and a Contradiction in Terms': Multiple-Use Forestry, Clearcutting, and the Politics of Fish Habitat in British Columbia, 1945-70." *BC Studies* 183 (Autumn 2014): 89–125.

Rajala, Richard. "'Streams Being Ruined from a Salmon-Producing Standpoint': Clearcutting, Fish Habitat, and Forest Regulation in British Columbia, 1900-45." *BC Studies* 176 (Winter 2012/13): 93-132.

Reksten, Terry. *The Dunsmuir Saga*. Vancouver: Douglas & McIntyre, 1994.

Scott, Christine. *Nature Strathcona: A Guide to Strathcona Park's 12 Nature Walks and Short Trails*. Calgary AB: Wilderness West Publications, 2007.

Searle, Rick. *Strathcona: British Columbia's First Provincial Park*. Produced in 2010. YouTube video, 18:22. https://www.youtube.com/watch?v=EAql-aPRghpw&feature=youtu.be.

Sefton MacDowell, Laura. *An Environmental History of Canada*. Vancouver: UBC Press, 2012.

Shilling, Grant. "Ruth Masters... Visions of Paradise, Eekology, Snafus, Boners and Belly Laughs." *The GIG*, April/May 2000. Susanne Lawson collection.

Siba, Catherine, Christine Dickinson, Deborah Griffiths and Judy Hagen. *Step into Wilderness: A Pictorial History of Outdoor Exploration in and around the Comox Valley*. Madeira Park, BC: Harbour Publishing, 2020.

Silkens, Thelma. "The Only Lord in America." *Musings* 25, no. 2 (May 2006).

Spaces For Nature. "Strathcona Provincial Park" (webpage). http://www.spacesfornature.org/greatspaces/strathcona.html. Accessed February 2018.

Stone, Philip. *Exploring Strathcona Park: A Guide to British Columbia's First Provincial Park*. Quathiaski Cove BC: WildIsle Publications, 2018.

Strathcona Park, Vancouver Island. Victoria: Department of Lands, 1921. Susanne Lawson collection.

Strathcona Wilderness Institute (website). http://strathconapark.org. Accessed March 12, 2017.

Taylor, W.A. *Crown Land Grants: A History of the Esquimalt and Nanaimo Railway Land Grants, the Railway Belt and the Peace River Block*. Victoria: Crown Land Registry Services, Ministry of Environment, Lands and Parks, 1975, 4th reprint 1997. Available online at https://ltsa.ca/wp-content/uploads/2020/10/Crown-Land-Grants-A-History-of-the-E-and-N.pdf

Tilden, Freeman. *Interpreting Our Heritage*. Chapel Hill: University of North Carolina Press, 1957, 1967.

Trew, D.M. *Reconnaissance Report on Strathcona Park including Forbidden Plateau*. Victoria: BC Forest Service, Parks Branch, 1950.

Tustin, Bob. *The History of Mountaineering on Vancouver Island: A Collection of Newspaper Stories, Journal Reports, Government Documents, Maps, Trip Write-Ups and Other Information Which Give Some Insight into Mountaineering on Vancouver Island*. Nanaimo: No publisher, 1984. Lindsay Elms collection.

Vancouver Island Trails Information Society. *Hiking Trails III: Central and Northern Vancouver Island and Quadra Island*. 7th ed. Revised and edited by Jim Rutter. Self-published, 1992.

Van Huizen, Philip. "'Panic Park': Environmental Protest and the Politics of Parks in British Columbia's Skagit Valley." *BC Studies* 170 (Summer 2011): 67–92.

Waiser, Bill. *Park Prisoners: The Untold History of Western Canada's National Parks, 1915–1946*. Saskatoon & Calgary: Fifth House Publishers, 1995.

Wilson, Jeremy. *Talk and Log: Wilderness Politics in British Columbia*. Vancouver: UBC Press, 1998.

Wilson, William H. "Reginald H. Thomson and Planning for Strathcona Park, 1912–15." *Planning Perspectives* 17, no. 4 (2002): 373–87.

Wood, Rob. *Towards the Unknown Mountain: An Autobiography from the Canadian Wilderness Frontier*. Campbell River BC: Ptarmigan Press, 1991.

Young, Paula. "Creating a 'Natural Asset': British Columbia's First Park, Strathcona, 1905–16." *BC Studies* 170 (Summer 2011): 17–39.

Archival Materials

Correspondence between Will J. Reid and Roderick Haig-Brown, 1939–1956. Box 16 File 1 and File 2. Roderick Haig-Brown fonds. University of British Columbia Library Rare Books and Special Collections. (Will J. Reid Foundation Founders' History Collection).

Inquisition Harry Linberg death of William McFarlane 1932. Gold River Historical Society, Gold River BC.

Laich-Kwil-Tach K'omoks Tlowitsis Council of Chiefs Traditional Use Project Archives, Dee Cullen Researcher, Thursday, accessed September 18, 2014. The Wei Wai Kum First Nation (Campbell River Indian Band, British Columbia) Archives, Campbell River, BC.

Masters, Ruth. "History of Forbidden Plateau." 1988. Courtenay and District Museum.

Minutes of Proceedings at Hearings Re: Application to Water Rights Branch for British Columbia By British Columbia Power Commission For: Permission to Erect a Dam at Buttle Lake, August 8, 9, 14, 15, 16, 17 and September 6, 1951. Will J. Reid Foundation Founders' History Collection. Also found in BC Archives GR-1236.

Resolutions Submitted by Campbell River and District Chamber of Commerce, Campbell River BC. Legislative Library of British Columbia, Victoria, BC, #333.78 C192.

Strathcona News/Province of British Columbia. Victoria: Ministry of Environment and Parks, Spring 1988. Legislative Library of British Columbia, Victoria BC # BC Periodicals.

Strathcona the Beautiful: Canada's Unrivalled National Park. Victoria: Bureau of Provincial Information, 1916. Legislative Library of British Columbia #BC B7B8 D:S7 1916.

Submission by the Campbell River District Pollution Control Society to the Pollution Control Board, concerning the addition of mine tailings into Buttle Lake, Strathcona Park, Vancouver Island (1968). Legislative Library of British Columbia #628.1683, 35.

Submissions 1988/Special Advisory Committee on Strathcona Park and Recreation Area, 1988. Legislative Library of British Columbia # BC S 722 D:S8 1988.

Thomson, R.H. *Third Annual Progress Report: Development of Strathcona Park.* Victoria: Department of Public Works, 1914. Legislative Library of British Columbia #917.11 S899aa, 17.

Personal Collections

Bordeville, Joe. Collection of newspaper articles and miscellaneous documents related to Will J. Reid.

Elms, Lindsay. Collection of newspaper articles, pamphlets and miscellaneous documents related to Strathcona Provincial Park.

Holmes, Margaret C. *Reginald H. Thomson*, Provincial Library, Exhibit X, British Columbia Power Commission for Permission to Erect a Dam at Buttle Lake, August 8, 9, 14, 15, 16, 17 and September 6, 1951. Will J. Reid Foundation Founders' History Collection also found in BC Archives GR-1236.

Lawson, Susanne. Collection of letters, newspaper articles, pamphlets and miscellaneous documents related to Strathcona Provincial Park.

Merilees, Bill. Series of taped interviews conducted with former Parks employees from 1997 to 2008.

Will J. Reid Family. Collection of correspondence, BC Water Rights Hearings Minutes 1951, Will Reid Nootka Lodge Log Book and numerous photos.

Interviews

Joe Bordeville, in telephone and email correspondence, since August 2018.

Jamie Boulding, Director, Strathcona Park Lodge and Outdoor Education Centre, in conversation with Catherine Gilbert, on several occasions from 2014 to 2020, Campbell River, BC.

Myrna Boulding, Founder, Strathcona Park Lodge and Outdoor Education Centre, in conversation with Catherine Gilbert, on several occasions from 2001 to 2020, Campbell River, BC.

Betty Brooks, interview with Catherine Gilbert, August 15 and 27, 2020, Black Creek, BC.

Ric Careless, Spaces for Nature, in discussion with Catherine Gilbert, February 10, 2018, Victoria, BC.

Ann Fiddick, former member of Strathcona Park Steering Committee, interview with Catherine Gilbert, December 12, 2017, Cedar, BC, and email correspondence, July through September, 2020.

David Garrick, chronicler of Greenpeace's first whale campaign, 1975, interview with Catherine Gilbert, October 26, 2020, Alert Bay, BC.

Owen Grant, Baseline Archaeology, in discussion with Catherine Gilbert, September 1, 2020, and subsequent email correspondence.

Mary Haig-Brown, daughter of Roderick Haig-Brown, interview with Catherine Gilbert, January 28, 2018, Victoria, BC, and email correspondence, July through September, 2020.

James Hancock, Zoom interview with Catherine Gilbert, May 30, 2020, Black Creek, BC.

Chester Lyons, interview with Bill Merilees, Tape 4A, October 14, 1996, from series of taped interviews conducted with former Parks employees from 1997 to 2008.

Bill Merilees, telephone interview with Catherine Gilbert, June 25, 2020, Black Creek, BC.

Jesse Morin, K'omoks First Nation, in discussion with Catherine Gilbert, September 25, 2020, Black Creek, BC.

Dr. Tom Pedersen, Professor of Marine Geochemistry at the University of Victoria, interview with Catherine Gilbert, December 17, 2017, Victoria, BC.

Elizabeth Purkiss, interview with Catherine Gilbert, December 22, 2020, Black Creek, BC.

Jim Rutter, former member of Strathcona Park Advisory Committee and Steering Committee, interview with Catherine Gilbert, November 24, 2017, Victoria, BC, and email correspondence, July through September 2020.

Sheila Savey Sr., Researcher Mowachaht/Muchalaht First Nation Evidence
    Gathering, email correspondence, September 2020.

Karen Schwalm, telephone interview with Catherine Gilbert, December 21,
    2017, Campbell River, BC, and in-person discussion and email correspon-
    dence, July through September 2020.

Andy Smith, Parks Area Supervisor, interview with Catherine Gilbert,
    September 9, 2020, Miracle Beach Headquarters, Black Creek, BC.

Marlene and Steve Smith, interview with Catherine Gilbert, September 8,
    2020, Merville, BC.

Teresa Strukoff, telephone interview with Catherine Gilbert, January 12, 2018,
    Victoria BC, and email correspondence, July through September 2020.

Chuck Symes, email correspondence with Catherine Gilbert, since January 2018.

Elizabeth Westbrook, interview with Catherine Gilbert, March 5, 2020, Black
    Creek, BC, and email correspondence to November 2020.

INDEX

Catherine Marie Gilbert is an author, historian and lecturer, whose interest in BC coastal life, past and present, is evident in her work. In 2018, she completed her master's thesis on the environmental history of Strathcona Provincial Park and obtained her masters degree in Public History from the University of Victoria. She is the author of *Yorke Island and the Uncertain War: Defending Canada's Western Coast*, and her articles have appeared in *Western Mariner*, BC *Historical Federation Journal*, BC *Studies* and *Escape*.